# Take It To Heart

**Crossway books by Christin Ditchfield**
*A Family Guide to Narnia*
*Take It To Heart*

SIXTY MEDITATIONS ON
GOD AND HIS WORD

# Take It To Heart

CHRISTIN DITCHFIELD

CROSSWAY BOOKS

A DIVISION OF
GOOD NEWS PUBLISHERS
WHEATON, ILLINOIS

**Library of Congress Cataloging-in-Publication Data**

Ditchfield, Christin.
   Take it to heart : a 60-day walk with God in his Word / Christin Ditchfield.
      p. cm.
   Includes bibliographical references.
   ISBN 1-58134-637-9
   1. Devotional calendars. I. Title.
BV4811.D55    2004
242'.2—dc22
                                    2004016324

| BP | | 14 | 13 | 12 | 11 | 10 | 09 | 08 | 07 | 06 | 05 |
|----|----|----|----|----|----|----|----|----|----|----|----|
| 15 | 14 | 13 | 12 | 11 | 10 | 9 | 8 | 7 | 6 | 5 | 4 | 3 | 2 | 1 |

To my father,
STEPHEN DITCHFIELD,


*who loves the Word of God with a greater passion
than anyone I've ever known. Thank you for sharing this
passion with me—speaking words of Scripture over me
at the very moment I was born, teaching me its truths
from my toddler years to my teens and beyond.
You continually impressed these commandments on my heart,
talking about them as we sat at home,
as we walked along the road, at bedtime and at breakfast
(Deuteronomy 6:6-7).
My life and ministry today is the fruit
of your labor of love.*

# SUPER STAIN REMOVER

These days it seems we're constantly being inundated with advertisements for cleaning products. With the incredible power of oxygen or citrus fruit or kickboxing chemical agents, they claim to remove "even the toughest stains" from any surface—under any circumstance. Some of these products really are rather remarkable. Too bad none of them can be taken internally. None of these amazing liquids or powders can make us feel clean inside. None of them can erase the wounds to our spirits, wipe away the mistakes of our past, or wash out the stain of our sin.

Like Lady Macbeth, we're desperate to rid ourselves of the telltale sign of our guilt. We try everything we can think of, all the products that promise to purify: denial, selective memory, rationalization, pointing the finger, or blaming others. We avoid people or situations that make us feel convicted. We do good works, hoping that they will somehow cancel out the bad ones. We go to elaborate lengths to cover up and hide our shame. Yet the stain remains.

When we finally reach the end of our own futile efforts, we fall on our faces before God, knowing we fully deserve His wrath and judgment—only to hear Him say, "Come now, let us reason together. . . . Though your sins are like scarlet, they shall be as white as snow" (Isaiah 1:18).

God applies His very own "super stain remover" to our hearts—the blood of Jesus, His Son. "If we confess our sins, he is faithful and just and will forgive us our sins and purify us from all unrighteousness" (1 John 1:9). The blood of Jesus gets out the most stubborn spots. It removes the darkest stains. It completely covers our guilt and shame and makes us pure again.

This most precious gift—our salvation—cost Jesus everything. Yet to us it's free if we receive it and believe in His name.

## Take It To Heart!

☞ Take a moment to search your heart. Is there unconfessed sin in your life? Do you struggle to believe that God can or will forgive you?

☞ Take God at His Word: Believe what the Scripture says; confess your sins and receive His forgiveness today.

☞ Read John 3:16-17 and Romans 8:1-2. You have probably read and heard these verses many times. Ask the Lord to help you see them with fresh eyes.

# CAN YOU SMELL HIM?

Sir Ralph Richardson once said, "If a man without a sense of smell declared that this yellow rose I hold had no scent, we should know that he was wrong. The defect is in him, not in the flower. It is the same with a man who says there is no God. It merely means that he is without the capacity to discern His presence."[1]

People who can't find any evidence of the existence of God just aren't looking—or don't know what they're looking at. Somehow it seems as if they're oblivious to His presence, completely unaware that His signature is written all over creation.

Romans 1:20 tells us that God has made it plain to them: "Since the creation of the world God's invisible qualities—his eternal power and divine nature—have been clearly seen, being understood from what has been made, so that men are without excuse."

No one is really unable to recognize the existence of God, but rather unwilling. God does everything He can to draw us into a relationship with Himself. He hasn't hidden from us. He wants us to know Him. God has revealed Himself in a myriad of ways: He's in the beauty of the sunset and the majesty of the mountains. He's in the roar of the ocean and in the soft and gentle breeze.

God speaks to us in visions and dreams, through the word of the prophets, and by the Word that became flesh and dwelt among us. May our hearts be ever attuned to His presence. May we clearly hear what He's saying to each one of us today.

## Take It To Heart!

𝕯 Take a moment to think of some times when you have sensed God's presence in a powerful way.

𝕯 Ask God to help you to be aware of Him working in and through your life today.

𝕯 Read Psalm 19:1-4 and Psalm 46:10. Make these verses your prayer for today.

# FORGIVE AND FORGET

Proverbs 19:11 says, "A man's wisdom gives him patience; it is to his glory to overlook an offense." When I first ran across that verse, it made me think of a story I once heard about a truly wise woman, Clara Barton—founder of the American Red Cross.

One day a friend reminded Clara of something awful that had been done to her in the past—a slight, an insult, a wound to her heart. But it appeared that Clara didn't recall the painful incident. "Don't you remember?" asked her astonished friend.

"No," Clara replied. "I distinctly remember forgetting it."[2]

Somehow Clara Barton understood that forgiveness isn't a feeling: It's a choice. And she chose to forgive the person who had offended her. It's not hard to understand why her friend was so surprised. After all, it's human nature to carry a grudge. But as any one who *has* held a grudge can tell you, it's pretty heavy baggage. We quickly find ourselves weighed down by anger, bitterness, resentment, and self-pity. The damage done to our spirit is often far worse than the immediate consequences of the original offense.

Sometimes we're carrying that baggage without realizing it. We say we've forgiven someone, and we may really think we have. But then we allow the painful memories to resurface again and again. We dwell on them constantly and experience the heartbreak new and fresh every time. We just can't understand why the pain won't go away.

Clara Barton refused to make that mistake. She refused to hang on to the hurt—reliving it over and over and over again. Instead, she chose to let it go. She made a conscious decision to forgive and forget. In doing so, Clara discovered the wonderful freedom that forgiveness brings. It's a freedom we, too, can experience when we choose to forgive.

## Take It To Heart!

℘ Take a moment to search your heart. Is there someone in your life that you need to forgive?

℘ Ask God to help you release any feelings of hurt or bitterness you have for the person. Choose to forgive today.

℘ Read Colossians 3:12-13 and Matthew 6:14-15.

# SERIOUSLY SEEKING HIM

In Lerner and Loewe's Broadway musical *My Fair Lady*, Professor Henry Higgins rants and raves against the "fairer sex." In the song "I'm An Ordinary Man," Higgins offers up a long list of complaints about his female acquaintances. In frustration he exclaims that a woman will "beg you for advice, your reply will be concise, and she'll listen very nicely, then go out and do precisely what she wants!"[3]

You know, he could be describing the way some of us approach our prayer life. We know we should seek God's will in a particular situation; so we make a point of spending some time in prayer. But—to be honest—we've already decided what we're going to do. We already have a plan. So once we've lingered on our knees for a "suitable" length of time, we jump up and head off to put our plan into action, confident that God will now bless our efforts. Then when things don't turn out the way we had hoped, we blame God for letting us down.

But lest we be confused, in Isaiah 55:8-9 God reminds us, "'My thoughts are not your thoughts, neither are your ways my ways,' declares the LORD. 'As the heavens are higher than the earth, so are my ways higher than your ways and my thoughts than your thoughts.'"

Our best-laid plans are often useless. We can't determine

the right course on our own. As Proverbs 14:12 observes, "There is a way that seems right to a man, but in the end it leads to death." If we seriously want to know the will of God, we need to approach Him in reverence and humility. If we truly want God to speak to us, we must leave our plans on the drawing board. We've got to be still in His presence—listening for His voice—with hearts that are willing to *do* whatever He *says*!

## Take It To Heart!

᷂ In what areas of your life do you need God's guidance today? Bring these concerns to Him in prayer, consciously releasing your own thoughts, plans, or ideas.

᷂ Open your heart to wherever God might lead. Listen for His voice throughout the day.

᷂ Read James 1:5-7 and Isaiah 30:18-21.

# HANNAH'S HEARTACHE

In the Old Testament we're introduced to a woman named Hannah. The Scripture says that she was barren, or childless, at a time when a woman's worth was measured by the number of children she produced. To be childless was a shame and an embarrassment, even a sign of God's disapproval. To make matters worse, Hannah's husband had another wife who had already given him many sons and daughters.

The Scripture says Hannah's husband loved her deeply, regardless of her inability to produce heirs. He went out of his way to give her preferential treatment in the family circle. But Hannah was heartbroken and would not be comforted by her husband's love. His other wife constantly gloated over her. First Samuel 1:7 tells us: "This went on year after year. Whenever Hannah went up to the house of the LORD, her rival provoked her till she wept and would not eat."

"Whenever she went up to the house of the LORD"—isn't that just like the enemy of our souls? At a time when we should be joyously anticipating an encounter with God, at a time when we have the opportunity to draw strength and comfort from His presence, Satan stirs up our deepest heartaches and fills our minds with painful memories of

14

offenses we've suffered. How often this happens as we're preparing for church, walking into the sanctuary, and slipping into the pew.

When we see how the enemy works, as we discover the strategies he uses to rob us of our peace and steal our joy, we can prepare for his attack. We can choose to ignore the evil things he whispers. We can refuse to dwell on the pain of the past. We can purposefully focus our thoughts on the truths of God's Word. If we hold fast to Him, we'll experience victory in Jesus' name.

## Take It To Heart!

🖎 Do you find yourself vulnerable to the enemy's attack at particular times or places? In specific areas of your life? Make a note of them.

🖎 Ask God to help you prepare a battle plan of your own. Think of some strategies you can use to stay on track.

🖎 Read Ephesians 6:10-18 and 2 Corinthians 10:4-5.

# THE POWER OF GENTLENESS

Do you remember the old fable about the contest between the wind and the sun? It seems they got into an argument over which one of them was the most powerful. An elderly man in a tattered coat came walking down the path. The wind challenged the sun to see which one of them could get the man's coat off.

Confident in his own strength, the wind went first. He began blustering and blowing with all his might, ripping at the edges of the tattered coat. But the poor old man ducked his head, hunched his shoulders, and pulled the coat more tightly to his chest.

When at last the mighty wind gave up, it was the sun's turn to shine. The sun slipped out from behind the clouds and beamed down on the old man so gently—and warmly— that the man immediately removed his coat and folded it over his arm.

This story always reminds me of the truth of Proverbs 15:1: "A gentle answer turns away wrath, but a harsh word stirs up anger." In our relationships with others, we often take an aggressive posture. Like the blustering wind, we try to win the point—or the argument—by overpowering and intimidating the other person. We blast him or her with the full force and strength of our sharpest words. But seldom does this approach produce the results we're looking for. Often we achieve the exact opposite!

The Scripture tells us there *is* a better way. Whether we're giving or receiving constructive criticism, settling an argument, or addressing a sensitive situation, we'd do well to remember the wisdom of Proverbs 15:1 and the power of a "gentle answer."

## Take It To Heart!

⌖ Can you think of a problem or circumstance in your life that was exacerbated by harsh words? How could it have been handled differently? What about a situation where a gentle answer saved the day?

⌖ Pray that God will give you gentle answers for the difficult people and circumstances that come into your life today.

⌖ Read James 3:3-18. Write down the areas that you need to work on.

# GOOD MORNING!

You may remember her as the bubbly sixteen-year-old gymnast who won a gold medal and touched the hearts of millions with her gutsy performance at the 1984 Olympic Games. Mary Lou Retton's "vault without fault" propelled her to superstar status in the international athletic community.

More than twenty years after her Olympic triumph, Mary Lou is still one of the most popular and widely recognized athletes in the world. She's also an accomplished and much sought-after TV commentator, author, and speaker—not to mention wife and mother of four preschool-aged daughters. Whenever she feels overwhelmed by the challenges of juggling all of her responsibilities, Mary Lou turns to a little piece of paper she has taped to her desk. It reads:

> *Good morning! This is God. I will be handling all of your problems today. I will not need your help. So relax and have a good day.*

"Isn't that great!" exclaims Retton. "I love it! That's what I try to live my day by, not stressing over the little things, the things that are out of our control. 'Cause we can worry ourselves sick. And worry is such a sin. Just give it to God!'"[4]

What a great reminder of the instruction we find in Psalm 55:22: "Cast your cares on the LORD and he will sustain you." It's so easy for us to get bogged down with worry and care and stressed out over all kinds of things that we have no control over. We need to bring all of our problems, all of our anxieties to our heavenly Father—and leave them in His care. He'll take care of them because He cares for us!

## Take It To Heart!

℘ Think about some of the things you have worried about unnecessarily—disasters that never happened or mountains that turned out to be molehills. List some specific occasions when God demonstrated His loving care for you.

℘ Now make a list of the things you're tempted to worry about today. Pray over each one and give it to God. Whenever the problem comes to mind, remember that it's in God's hands. (To help you remember, you might make your own sign like the one Mary Lou keeps on her desk. Put it in a place where you will see it often.)

℘ Read Philippians 4:4-7 and 1 Peter 5:6-7. Memorize some of these verses so that you can recall them when you begin to worry.

# THE SCHOOL OF LIFE

When I was a young child, I loved school. I loved to learn. I loved to go shopping for brand-new school supplies. But as I grew older, I joined my classmates in counting the days—and years—till we would be "free." We couldn't wait to grow up and get on with life. We had no idea that life itself is one giant classroom in the school of hard knocks. Our graduation day would hardly mark the end of our education. It was just the beginning.

If only we knew then what we know now. Raise your hand if you would have worked a little harder in school or paid more attention to those skills you were sure you would never need in "real life."

You know, it's true in a spiritual sense, too—that all of life is a school. We graduate when we pass from this life to the next. As my grandfather likes to say, he's "cramming for his finals." Which brings me to my point: Instead of merely marking time, we all need to be hitting the books—or *the* Book.

See, we're all students in the classroom of life, and God Himself is our Teacher. We can't afford to waste time staring out the window, waiting for recess. We've been given this precious time to get to know God here and now, so that we will know Him better in eternity. This is our opportunity to

learn and grow in our faith. We undergo trials—or tests—
that produce character and develop our maturity. But when
the bell rings, class is over. Time is up. Who we have become
is who we will be for all eternity. The psalmist prayed,
"Teach us to number our days aright, that we may gain a
heart of wisdom" (Psalm 90:12).

## Take It To Heart!

⚅ Think about it: Are you living life to the fullest, taking advantage of every opportunity to learn and grow and
mature in your faith. Or are you simply passing time?

⚅ Pray for wisdom. Ask God to show you where to
direct your energy and efforts, and how to make the most of
the time He's given you.

⚅ Read Matthew 25:1-29 and Ephesians 5:15-20.
What do these verses teach you about using your time on
earth?

# NEVER FORGOTTEN

Have you ever been forgotten? When you were a kid, did your parents ever accidentally leave you at the gas station or the restaurant? Was there a time when each one thought the other one had picked you up from school? Were you left off the invitation list to a special party? Ignored by others in a social setting, at church, or at work?

There's no question that at some point or another we've all experienced the pain of feeling abandoned, neglected, or unloved—times when even God seemed far away. The Old Testament describes an occasion when God's people experienced that same kind of pain. Isaiah 49:14 tells us, "Zion said, 'The LORD has forsaken me, the Lord has forgotten me.'"

But God answered, "'Can a woman forget the baby at her breast and have no compassion on the child she has borne? Though she may forget, I will not forget you! See, I have engraved you on the palms of my hands.'"

*"I have engraved you on the palms of my hands."* Some translations of this Scripture say "inscribed," "tattooed," or "indelibly imprinted." What a powerful picture of the steadfast love the Lord has for us. Others may forget us or ignore us or leave us off the list. Others may abandon us. But our heavenly Father never will. Because of His love for us, we are never forsaken. We are never forgotten.

In the New Testament, Jesus gave us this precious promise, "Surely I am with you always, to the very end of the age" (Matthew 28:20). Let these words bring comfort and assurance to your heart today.

## Take It To Heart!

🍵 Have you felt alone or abandoned lately? Have experiences in your past made you vulnerable to fear or resentment?

🍵 Ask God to help you experience the reality of His presence. Memorize Scriptures that remind you of His faithfulness and repeat them often.

🍵 Read Psalm 91 and Psalm 145:18. What encouragement can you draw from these passages?

# THE WORDS OF A
# WISE WOMAN

Proverbs 18:21 says, "The tongue has the power of life and death. . . ." Over and over the Scriptures remind us to guard our lips and choose our words carefully because words are powerful. They change hearts and minds. They change history. The Bible gives us an example in 1 Samuel 25.

David was enraged when a foolish man snubbed him, ridiculed him, and publicly insulted him. The man who would be king gathered his army and prepared to launch a full-scale attack on the ignorant peasant farmer. But the farmer had a wife, Abigail, whom the Scripture describes as "an intelligent and beautiful woman." She bravely rode out to meet David in the hopes of averting disaster. She brought him gifts—and wise council.

Abigail started by acknowledging the call of God on David's life and his right to be angry over her husband's foolishness. Then she reminded David that the *Lord* would fight his battles and deal with his enemies. She also reminded him that there would be a consequence for the sin he was planning to commit. Abigail urged David to ignore her husband and instead focus on his own destiny as Israel's next king. She said that then, "When the LORD . . . has appointed him leader over Israel, my master will not have on his conscience the staggering burden of needless bloodshed or of having avenged himself" (1 Samuel 25:30-31).

David listened to the words of this wise woman and did what was right. And God avenged him. Think what might have happened if Abigail had not had the courage to speak up! Or worse, if she had heaped fuel on the fire and encouraged David to destroy her foolish husband. "The tongue has the power of life and death." As Abigail's story shows us, it's imperative that we use our tongues wisely.

## Take It To Heart!

🖎 Think of the people in your life that you have the opportunity to influence. When you give them advice, is it founded on Scripture? Do you point them to back to God?

🖎 Ask God to give you wisdom and discernment. Pray for direction before you give advice to others.

🖎 Read Psalm 141:3; Proverbs 9:10; 12:18; 15:28; 1 Peter 4:11a.

# Fresh Bread

As the children of Israel began their wilderness wanderings, they grumbled and complained that God had brought them out of slavery in Egypt, only to let them starve in the desert. Then God, in His mercy, provided for them by sending manna—bread from heaven. This miraculous food was like nothing they had ever seen, which it is why they called it manna, meaning "what is it?" Every day it appeared on the ground like the dew. "Each morning everyone gathered as much as he needed" (Exodus 16:21). And they were fed.

But there was one thing about the manna—it didn't keep. They couldn't store it up and save it for a rainy day. The Israelites had to gather a fresh supply every morning. They had to look to God for His provision each new day.

We may not be wandering through the wilderness, but we are all on a journey of faith. The same God who led Israel leads us today. When we've gone some distance, we find we can look back and remember His miraculous provision in many circumstances and on numerous occasions. We may even recall specific lessons He taught us, certain things He spoke so clearly to our hearts.

But if we're not careful, we can find ourselves leaning a little too heavily on the "glory days" gone by. We become content to regurgitate the things we learned years ago—when our heavenly Father has so much more to teach us, so much more to say! There's no need to chew on stale bread. God has a fresh Word to give us each day.

In Psalm 81:10, He says, "I am the LORD your God, who brought you up out of Egypt. Open wide your mouth and I will fill it."

Are you hungry for the things of God? If not, ask Him to give you that hunger. Take time now to quiet your heart before Him. Read His Word, talk to Him in prayer—and listen. He has something new to say to you today.

## Take It To Heart!

🦋 Think about your schedule over the past few days or weeks. Have you been making time to seek God? Do you look to Him for strength for each new day? If not, what changes could you make to spend quality time with God.

🦋 Ask God to speak to you or teach you something new today. Keep your eyes and ears open. He may answer you in a surprising way!

🦋 Read Psalm 63:1-5 and Matthew 6:6.

# EINSTEIN AND THE CHURCH

Albert Einstein was not a Christian, but he made a remarkable observation about the church during the time of Hitler and the Nazis in World War II. Einstein wrote:

> Having always been an ardent partisan of freedom, I turned to the universities . . . to find there the defenders of freedom. I did not find them. Very soon the universities took refuge in silence. I then turned to the editors of powerful newspapers, who, but lately in flowing articles, had claimed to be the faithful champions of liberty. These men, as well . . . were reduced to silence within a few weeks. I then addressed myself to the authors individually, to those who passed themselves off as the intellectual guides of Germany . . . [who] had frequently discussed the question of freedom and its place in modern life. They were in their turn silent.
>
> Only the Church opposed the fight which Hitler was waging against liberty. Till then I had no interest in the Church, but now I feel great admiration [for] and am truly attracted to the Church which had the persistent courage to fight for spiritual truth and moral freedom. . . . I now admire what I used to consider of little value.[5]

Wow! When I first read that powerful statement, I felt proud to be a Christian, thrilled to share a heritage with those who wholeheartedly obeyed the words of 1 Corinthians

16:13: "Be on your guard; stand firm in the faith; be men of courage; be strong."

Then I couldn't help but wonder if Einstein would be able to make the same observation today. If he looked at the church today, would he see us bravely standing in the face of evil, refusing to surrender our moral values and principles, fighting for truth and righteousness? It's a sobering thought—one we all need to consider as we strive to live out the faith we profess.

## Take It To Heart!

✍ What are the cultural issues and world crises confronting us today? How is the church responding? How are you personally responding?

✍ Ask God to show you where and how He would have you take a stand—or join the fight. You may need to make some changes in your lifestyle. You may need to take a more active role in your family, church, or community. Pray for wisdom.

✍ Read Proverbs 24:10-12 and Isaiah 1:17.

# HE UNDERSTANDS

There are few things in life as irritating as advice from people who don't know what they're talking about. They've never had the kind of problems we have, never had to face what we face. But that doesn't keep them from offering their expert opinions.

You know what I mean: suggestions on how to manage your finances from people who've always had a steady paycheck and never had a hard time making ends meet. Or how about tips on how to parent your strong-willed child from people whose children are all compliant, eager to obey. Then there are those helpful comments on dieting from naturally thin people who have never even been tempted to overeat.

These people just don't get it. They don't understand why something so simple to them can be such a struggle for us. They have never felt our pain, battled our addiction, or overcome the kind of obstacles constantly thrown in our path. Consequently, they're not much help. They're certainly not sympathetic. But Jesus is.

Hebrews 4:15-16 says that we can come to Him with all of our problems, our struggles with sin, our most trying circumstances: "For we do not have a high priest who is unable to sympathize with our weaknesses, but we have one who has been tempted in every way, just as we are—yet was without sin. Let us then approach the throne of grace with confidence, so that we may receive mercy and find grace to help us in our time of need."

Jesus knows all about the challenges we face. He really does understand what we're going through. He *has* experienced temptation and overcome it! He can lead us to victory if we'll take up our cross and follow Him (Luke 9:23).

## Take It To Heart!

✍ Do you ever feel alone in your struggles—as if no one really understands what you're going through?

✍ Bring these thoughts and feelings to God, along with your problems. Thank Him that He hears your heart. Ask Him to give you victory in every area of your life.

✍ Read Psalm 103:13-14; James 4:6; 1 Corinthians 10:13.

# WHO'S THE BOSS?

You can see it in the proliferation of cartoons and bumper stickers, the popularity of T-shirts and coffee mugs that proclaim:

*I hate Mondays.*
*Can I trade this job for what's behind Door Number Two?*
*I work 40 hours a week to be this poor!*
*A cubicle is a padded cell without a door.*

Unfortunately, many of us feel taken advantage of by our employers—or our families. We're overworked, underpaid, and unappreciated. As our frustration grows, we start to get bitter and resentful. We complain to anyone who will listen, and we nurse what will soon become the mother-of-all bad attitudes. Our performance suffers because—let's face it—we're having trouble finding the motivation to get out of bed, let alone give our best effort. And why should we? The ungrateful people we work for don't deserve it.

But Colossians 3:23-24 tells us that as believers, we answer to a higher authority. We're called to a different standard. Paul writes, "Whatever you do, work at it with all your heart, as working for the Lord, not for men, since you know that you will receive an inheritance from the Lord as a reward. It is the Lord Christ you are serving."

Uh-oh. Maybe it's time for an attitude adjustment! We need to remember that as Christians everything we do is an act of service to God. He is the one who will reward our efforts. Whether we're driving a truck or doing dishes, answering phones or processing paperwork, let's do our best to make our Boss proud!

## Take It To Heart!

۞ So how is your attitude at work? Whatever your job may be, are you following the biblical directive to "work at it with all your heart"? Are you giving your best effort?

۞ Ask God to help you remember that you work for Him. When you're tempted to complain about or criticize those in your workplace, pray for them instead.

۞ Read Ephesians 6:5-8 and 1 Peter 2:13-23.

# DID YOU SAY SOMETHING?

In the classic allegory *The Pilgrim's Progress*, author John Bunyan describes the journey of a man named Christian who travels from sin and bondage in the City of Destruction to eternal peace and joy in the Celestial City. Along the way Christian faces many trials that test his faith. There are many obstacles to overcome.

At one point Christian passes through a dark valley inhabited by hideous demonic beings. These evil creatures hover about, just out of sight. Then they begin to whisper the most awful, blasphemous things in Christian's ear. Stumbling along in the dark, Christian can't see the demons. He mistakes their voices for his own thoughts. Christian is overcome with horror and shame and self-reproach. How could he think such things? What a terrible wretch he is! He staggers under the guilt and despair.

Down through the ages, many believers have experienced that very same thing. Satan whispers his blasphemies, introduces evil thoughts—and we're shocked and dismayed. We think *we* came up with these vile expressions. We ask ourselves, "Can I really be a Christian and think such a thing?" We feel defeated in our walk with Christ. Some of us even begin to doubt our salvation.

In Bunyan's story, Christian is rescued when a friend comes alongside him and begins quoting the Word of God. Just as the Scripture promises, the demonic beings are forced to flee. You know, the same strategy will work for us today.

So often we mistake the voice of the enemy for that of our own hearts. We feel guilty and ashamed and question our salvation—when what we need to do is follow the admonition of James 4:7: "Resist the devil, and he will flee from you." It's time we stop taking credit for the devil's filth, refuse to listen to his lies, and determine to counter every blasphemous thought with the Scriptures, words of truth and praise.

## Take It To Heart!

🍃 What evil things has the enemy whispered in your ear? How do you usually respond?

🍃 Think of a Scripture or song of praise that you can use to counter the devil's filth. Repeat this verse—or sing this song—throughout the day, whenever you feel tempted to succumb to the enemy's attack. Ask a friend to pray for you.

🍃 Read Genesis 3:1-6; John 8:44b; Matthew 4:1-11.

# WHEN YOUR DREAMS
# DON'T COME TRUE

When Michelle was a little girl, she had a dream. It was no ordinary dream—it was a *big* dream! She wanted to be a wide receiver for the Pittsburgh Steelers. She wore her "Mean Joe Green" Steelers jersey every day. She practiced making "Hail Mary" catches in the backyard with her father and brother. Then one day a well-meaning teacher took little Michelle aside and told her the cold, hard truth: "Girls don't play football!"

Michelle was crushed. Her dream was shattered. But in the years that followed, she would come to understand the truth of Jeremiah 29:11: "'For I know the plans I have for you,' declares the LORD, 'plans to prosper you and not to harm you, plans to give you hope and a future.'"

God had given Michelle all that athletic ability for a reason. He had a plan all along. Little did she know, but one day Michelle Akers would have the opportunity to glorify Him before millions as "the greatest female soccer player in the world."

After leading the United States women's soccer team to their first gold medal at the 1996 Olympics in Atlanta, Michelle reflected on all the obstacles she had faced in the past—the disappointments, the heartbreaks, the serious health problems. She wrote in her journal:

> *The past few years, I thought I was so alone, so isolated in my struggles and pain. But God is so good. Through it all, He was preparing me for this moment, this experience. So faithful! He took it all away, but He gave me back so much more.*[6]

If your life hasn't turned out the way you wanted it to, if like Michelle, you've suffered the death of a dream, don't be discouraged. Surrender the dream to God. Let Him reveal His plan, His purpose for you. It will far exceed anything you can imagine. Just ask Michelle!

## Take It To Heart!

🕉 What dreams have not come true for you? Can you see God's hand at work in spite of your disappointments?

🕉 Take a moment now to affirm your trust in Him. Ask God to lead you to the dreams He has for you.

🕉 Read Psalm 139:1-16 and Proverbs 3:5-6.

# Not Too Proud

There comes a day in every toddler's life when he or she will push away a parent's hand, refuse assistance with the spoon or the sweater, and announce to the world, "I can do it myself!" That declaration of independence is an important step in a child's development. But unfortunately some of us never get past it. Well into adulthood, we're still trying to assert ourselves and prove our abilities.

You know, it takes wisdom and maturity to admit that there are some things we *can't* do ourselves—to acknowledge that there will always be circumstances in which we need help.

The book of Exodus tells of a time when Moses was struggling to cope with all the responsibilities that came with leading the nation of Israel. His father-in-law Jethro visited the camp and saw at once that Moses was exhausted. There the man of God sat—from sunup to sundown—listening to people's complaints, solving problems, and settling disputes.

Jethro told him it was not right: "The work is too heavy for you; you cannot handle it alone" (Exodus 18:18). He told Moses that his time could be better spent. There were more effective ways for him to serve God and the people. Jethro advised Moses to delegate his authority and responsibilities by sharing them with other capable men who were called by God to assist him.

How did his son-in-law respond to this unsolicited advice? The Scripture says, "Moses listened to his father-in-law and did everything he said" (Exodus 18:24). Though he was one of the most influential leaders in history, one of the greatest men ever to walk the earth, Moses was not too proud or stubborn to admit he needed help.

We can learn a lot from his example.

## Take It To Heart!

☞ Do you feel overwhelmed by the demands of your schedule? Are you trying to do everything yourself? Does your current strategy truly maximize your efforts and make the best use of your time and talents?

☞ Ask God to show you what things to delegate (and to whom), what things to reschedule or reorganize, and what things to let go. Look to Him for direction as you reassess your priorities.

☞ Read Romans 12:3-8 and 1 Peter 5:5-7.

# It Hurts Him More
# Than It Hurts Us

We've all chuckled over the expression of a parent who says, as he is about to discipline a child, "This is going to hurt me a lot more than it hurts you." When you're a kid, that statement seems so ludicrous. But when you become an adult, you begin to understand just how difficult and unpleasant—even painful—it can be to have to inflict discipline on those precious little ones in your care. It's just awful to watch them suffer. How deeply you wish you didn't have to go through with it. If only they would obey!

You know, there are times when our heavenly Father has to discipline us. Sometimes He must allow us to suffer the painful consequences of our disobedience so that we'll have the opportunity to learn from our mistakes.

Lamentations 3:32-33 says, "Though he brings grief, he will show compassion, so great is his unfailing love. For he does not willingly bring affliction or grief to the children of men."

As a loving parent, God is never gleeful about disciplining us. It doesn't amuse Him to see us grapple with pain and heartbreak. On the contrary, it grieves Him deeply. But He loves us so much that He's willing to allow us to hurt, so that we'll learn and be motivated to change. Then maybe the next time, we'll obey. And we won't have to suffer the consequences of disobedience again and again.

If God has been disciplining you lately, if you find yourself experiencing the painful consequences of disobedience in your past, make a decision: Receive the correction. Choose to learn from the experience. Don't run *from* God in your pain—run *to* Him. Confess your sin, receive His forgiveness, and experience His amazing grace!

## Take It To Heart!

🕮 Think of some of the important lessons you have learned from discipline in the past—from your parents or teachers or employers.

🕮 Thank God that He loves you too much to leave you the way you are. Ask Him to help you respond positively to His discipline and correction. Determine to mature and grow in your faith.

🕮 Read Psalm 119:71 and Hebrews 12:4-11.

# IN THE GARDEN TOMB

Several years ago I had the privilege of touring the Holy Land with a group of Christian women journalists. It was truly an incredible experience. So many familiar Scriptures took on new meaning as we were able to put them into cultural, historical, and geographical context. But by far, the most meaningful experience for me was our brief visit to the Garden Tomb in Jerusalem.

So many of the traditional "religious" sites we visited were dark and dismal places—shrouded by centuries of religious superstition and empty ritual worship. In order to believe that the place was what it claimed to be, one would have to completely disregard the biblical account of what supposedly took place there—or twist the Scriptures to make it fit—accepting the traditions of men over the truth of the Word.

But in the peaceful beauty of the Garden Tomb, it was a different story. The chaplain led us from place to place around the garden, sharing the Scriptures with us and pointing out how in every respect what we were looking at matched the biblical account perfectly. "This is what the Bible says . . . and this is what we find." It was so simple and beautiful and faith-affirming.

Our tour ended at the tomb itself. After explaining traditional burial customs and reminding us of the description of this place in the Gospels, our guide concluded: "But you know, you've come all this way to see nothing. The tomb is empty. My Jesus is not here. He is risen just as He said."

Hallelujah! Our hope is not in pilgrimages to sacred sites, ancient altars, and man-made monuments. Our faith is built on the reality of the Resurrection. Our trust is in our risen Savior, Jesus Christ our Lord.

## Take It To Heart!

✐ Think about the Resurrection: what it means to our faith, what it means to you personally. How would you explain it to an unbeliever? It might help to write your thoughts on paper.

✐ Spend a few moments in praise and worship. Rejoice in your risen Savior!

✐ Read Matthew 28:1-9 and 1 Corinthians 15:1-22.

# OUT LIKE A LIGHT

In the days after Jesus' death and resurrection, the good news of the gospel spread like wildfire. The early church grew at an alarming rate—alarming at least to its enemies. It was then that the church began to suffer state-sponsored persecution. Many of Jesus' disciples were imprisoned, tortured, and executed for their faith.

At one point King Herod arrested Simon Peter, planning to bring him to trial after the Passover. Herod had him guarded by a squad of sixteen men. Peter was chained between two of the soldiers around the clock. But regardless of Herod's evil plans, it simply wasn't Peter's time to go. God still had work for him to do. So the night before the trial, "an angel of the Lord appeared and a light shone in the cell. He struck Peter on the side and woke him up. 'Quick, get up!' he said, and the chains fell off Peter's wrists" (Acts 12:7).

Does anything about that scenario strike you as a bit odd—besides the angelic visitation, I mean? Think about it. If you were in a prison cell, knowing you would likely be executed in the morning, what would you be doing? Anxiously pacing the floor? Wringing your hands? Crying out to God in fear and desperation? Or sleeping so soundly someone would have to hit you to wake you up?

How did he do it? How could Peter sleep at a time like

that? In a word, trust. Peter trusted God utterly and completely. He knew his life was in the hands of his heavenly Father. One way or another, things would turn out all right. If he lived, God would be with him. If he died, he'd be with God. Either way, it was okay with him. When you live with that perspective, you can sleep through anything!

## Take It To Heart!

🅑 Think about it: Do you believe that God is in control of everything that happens to you? Do you believe that He loves you? Do you trust Him?

🅑 Thank God for His faithfulness. Ask Him to help you keep the trials and tribulations of this life in perspective. Affirm your trust in Him.

🅑 Read Isaiah 26:3 and Romans 8:28-39.

# LITTLE FOXES

If you've ever done much gardening, you know that in addition to choosing what to plant and when—and aside from nurturing new growth and providing adequate water and sunlight—one of the most critical tasks is to keep the pests away. You've got to protect the tender plant from being trampled or eaten by its enemies, be they bug or bird or beast.

Did you know that the same is true for the garden of our hearts? In John 15:5 Jesus said, "I am the vine; you are the branches. If a man remains in me and I in him, he will bear much fruit." Further on in the chapter, He said again, "I chose you and appointed you to go and bear fruit—fruit that will last" (v. 16). If we abide in the vine, He will provide all the nutrients—all the nurturing—we need. But it's our job to keep away the pests.

Song of Songs 2:15 says, "Catch for us the foxes, the little foxes that ruin the vineyards, our vineyards that are in bloom." Are there any "little foxes" in your garden today? Inappropriate thoughts that have gone unchecked? Bad habits that have taken root? Small sins you secretly make allowance for?

The trouble with little foxes is that they don't look dangerous from the outset. They hardly even seem a threat. But these pesky critters nibble at the vine and destroy our life-giving connection to God. They quickly devour the fruit He has so patiently labored to produce in our lives. The guilt and hypocrisy alone is enough to cripple us and keep us from experiencing meaningful fellowship with the Lord.

If you see any "little foxes" in the garden of your heart, don't be deceived by their harmless appearance. Catch them now before they grow into monsters. Protect your precious fruit.

## Take It To Heart!

✍ Take a few moments to examine your heart. Are there any "little foxes" there? What are they? When did they arrive?

✍ Confess these sins to God. Take action immediately to remove them from your heart and life. It might be helpful to ask a trusted friend to hold you accountable.

✍ Read James 1:14-15 and 1 Corinthians 10:12-13.

# AMERICAN IDOLS

I know I'm going to date myself here, but I was in high school when they first launched the "Just Say No" to drugs campaign. And they went at it full throttle. "Just Say No" was everywhere—T-shirts, bumper stickers, school assemblies, and after-school clubs and activities.

About the same time, during school-spirit week, they told us to come to class in costume. For fun we could dress up as one of two "American idols": Elvis Presley or Marilyn Monroe. Both of those people died of drug overdoses. Talk about sending a mixed message!

Sad to say, that's the case with far too many American idols. These celebrities drink and do drugs, dress like prostitutes, lust after riches, live to excess, boast of their bad behavior, and show contempt for authority and disregard for the feelings and welfare of others. And yet society holds them up to our children as role models.

Even adults find themselves wanting to imitate the look or lifestyle of these popular celebrities or copy the strategies of the super-wealthy, super-successful business tycoons. But following their example will only bring us the same emptiness and heartache, the same disappointment and devastation, the same judgment as these people ultimately experience.

The Scriptures warn us not to imitate what is evil: "Don't let this bad example influence you. Follow only what is good. Remember that those who do good prove that they are God's children, and those who do evil prove that they do not know God" (3 John 11 NLT). James urges us: "Get rid of all moral filth and the evil that is so prevalent and humbly accept the word planted in you, which can save you" (James 1:21). And the apostle Paul writes, "Follow God's example in everything you do" (Ephesians 5:1 NLT).

## Take It To Heart!

꿈 Who are your role models? Why? What kind of person would you really like to be? Can you think of any godly examples you aspire to?

꿈 Thank God for those who have been positive influences in your life. Pray that He will help you to imitate what is good, that you in turn may be a godly role model for others.

꿈 Read Romans 12:1-2; Ephesians 5:1-2; 1 Timothy 4:12.

# STONES FROM THE JORDAN

As Joshua led the children of Israel into the Promised Land, God did many amazing and wondrous things to demonstrate His power and love. He was showing them that He was with them and that He would bless them in the new land. When the people arrived at the banks of the Jordan River, it was harvest time, and the river was at its fullest. But as the priests carrying the Ark of the Covenant stepped into the water at the river's edge, the flow of water miraculously ceased. It was cut off upstream, and all the people were able to walk across the riverbed as if it were dry land.

While the priests stood there, Joshua sent the leaders of the twelve tribes back to the riverbed, commanding each of them to gather a large stone. "We will use these stones to build a memorial," he said. "In the future, when your children ask you, 'What do these stones mean?' tell them that the flow of the Jordan was cut off before the ark of the covenant of the LORD. When it crossed the Jordan, the waters of the Jordan were cut off. These stones are to be a memorial to the people of Israel forever" (Joshua 4:6-7).

You know, people all over the world still build memorials today. A memorial is a way to remember something precious or sacred, something historic, something vitally important to us. It's a wonderful tradition each of us can carry on in our own hearts and with our own families.

When God does something miraculous in your life, take time to "build" a memorial. Do something special to create a memory of the experience. Write it down in a letter or journal or scrapbook. Tell the story to your friends and family—especially to your children and grandchildren. Relive the experience over and over in your heart so that you'll never forget what the Lord has done for you.

## Take It To Heart!

✍ Take a moment now to remember two or three spiritually significant events in your life. Relive them in your heart and mind.

✍ Give thanks to God for His awesome power and amazing love. Ask Him for an opportunity to share a story of His faithfulness with someone in your life today.

✍ Read Psalm 71:15-18 and Psalm 77:11-14.

# CAN I GET A LITTLE SALT WITH THAT?

One summer when I was a teenager, I worked as a waitress at a family-friendly restaurant. I was pretty nervous my first day. But once I got the hang of it, it wasn't too hard. And the pay was pretty good. There was just one thing I really hated about the job: the behavior of some of our customers.

From the moment they walked through the door, these people were critical and condescending, rude to the staff. They didn't like where they were seated. The menu didn't offer what they wanted. The prices were too high. These customers complained about everything. Then when their food arrived, they would all join hands ceremoniously and pray loudly—so as to be a "witness."

It was too late for that. No matter how powerful the prayer, it couldn't undo the damage of the caustic words that preceded it. Time after time I watched my coworkers head back to the kitchen, grumbling about these obnoxious "Christian people." I didn't know what to say myself.

In Colossians 4:5-6, the apostle Paul says, "Be wise in the way you act toward outsiders; make the most of every opportunity. Let your conversation be always full of grace, seasoned with salt, so that you may know how to answer everyone."

Salt is a preservative. It enhances the flavor of food. It makes you thirsty.

Did you know that our words can have the same effect? We can speak in a way that inspires and encourages others. We can be so polite and warm and friendly that unbelievers actually enjoy talking with us. Something in the way we speak refreshes them and at the same time makes them "thirsty" for more. Then when we share with them the "reason for the hope that [we] have"—when we tell them about Jesus—they're listening (1 Peter 3:15).

Is your conversation "full of grace" and "seasoned with salt"? The next time you go out to eat, wait in line at the bank, or stop for gas, choose to "be wise," as Paul said, and make the most of every opportunity. Say something "salty" that could change people's lives and impact them for all eternity.

## Take It To Heart!

☞ If unbelievers listened to the way you speak to the staff at your local restaurant, bank, or grocery store, would they be able to tell that you are a Christian? Do you sound like someone they might want to get to know?

☞ Pray that God will help you live out your testimony in word *and* deed. Look for opportunities to engage in conversations that are "full of grace" and "seasoned with salt."

☞ Read James 3:3-10 and Psalm 19:14.

# Paul's Workout

When you're young, you're full of energy. You can run and play and even work for hours on end without getting noticeably tired. But as you get older, your energy starts to fade. Your body slows down. Soon you discover the truth in the popular expression: "If you don't use it, you lose it." Without regular exercise, you will be constantly out of breath and out of shape!

You know, the same thing is true on a spiritual level. When we're new believers, young in the faith, we're full of energy and life. We're enthusiastic about reading the Word, praying, and fellowshipping with other believers. We look for ways to share the gospel with our friends and neighbors. We work hard to overcome patterns of sinful behavior from our past, and we develop new habits—spiritual disciplines— that strengthen our walk with Christ. In the race of faith, we're intent on "pressing on to win the prize."

But as the years go by, some of us find that our enthusiasm comes and goes. It's easy to get distracted and forget the goal. We get sidetracked; we relax our standards. We let go of those spiritual disciplines we developed, and we resume some of our old habits. Before we know it, we're huffing and puffing—out of shape spiritually.

In 1 Corinthians 9:26-27, the apostle Paul said, "I do not

run like a man running aimlessly; I do not fight like a man beating the air. No, I beat my body and make it my slave so that after I have preached to others, I myself will not be disqualified. . . ."

Those of us who are mature believers should take note—and take care to stay on track spiritually. We can't be resting on our laurels when there's a race to be run. We've got to keep disciplining ourselves, keep exercising and strengthening our spiritual muscles. Let's take our cue from Paul: Do whatever it takes to stay in shape and win the prize!

## Take It To Heart!

✍ What kind of shape are you in today? How does your spiritual life compare to what it was a few months ago? A few years ago?

✍ Come up with some ways you can strengthen your spirit today. Ask God to guide you as you set some spiritual goals. Then ask Him to help you meet them.

✍ Read 1 Timothy 4:7b-8; Philippians 3:12-14; Hebrews 12:1-3.

# LEAH'S LEGACY

Remember the story of Rachel and Leah in the Bible? Jacob was very much in love with Rachel, but was tricked into marrying her older sister Leah first. The two sisters constantly competed for their husband's love and attention. Leah was the loser right from the start. Jacob had never loved or wanted her. Rachel now deeply resented her.

Genesis 29:31 says the Lord saw that Leah was not loved—and He had compassion on her. He gave her children, something Rachel couldn't have. Leah was thrilled. She thought that by producing Jacob's first heir, she would somehow earn his love and respect. She cried, "The LORD has seen my misery. Surely my husband will love me now." At the birth of her second son, Leah said, "Because the LORD heard that I am not loved, he gave me this one too." When her third son was born, Leah said, "Now at last my husband will become attached to me, because I have borne him three sons." But Jacob's feelings for Leah never changed.

Many of us can identify with Leah's heartbreak. Our circumstances are different, but we, too, have experienced the pain of rejection. We have tried everything we could think of, done everything we could do, jumped through hoops—only to discover as Leah did that you can't make someone love you.

With the birth of her fourth son, Leah had a revelation. She said simply, "This time I will praise the LORD."

The truth is that there's just no point in trying to earn love and acceptance from those unwilling or unable to give it. The effort only leaves us frustrated, exhausted, empty, and depressed. God says He has loved us with an everlasting love, that we are precious to Him. We've got to stop looking to others for approval or affirmation. Instead, we need to turn to our heavenly Father and say, "This time I will praise the Lord."

## Take It To Heart!

✍ Do you find yourself trying to win others' acceptance, approval, or love? Why? Does someone in your life make you feel unworthy of love and respect?

✍ Make a decision: "Today I will choose to focus on the truth of God's wonderful love for me." Spend a few moments praising Him right now.

✍ Read Psalm 108:1-4 and Romans 8:31-39.

# JUST ASK!

It's a common complaint of women everywhere: Men are forever getting lost because they won't stop and ask for directions. To be perfectly fair, I think it's an affliction that affects both sexes. Women may be quick to buy a map for a road trip, but there are plenty of other projects we plunge into—only to find ourselves in over our heads. And just like the guys, we refuse to ask for help.

Why is that? Why are we all so reluctant to ask for guidance and direction when we need it? Maybe it's because we're in denial—we won't admit that we have a problem. Sometimes we're embarrassed about it. We don't want anyone to think we're stupid. Other times we're so busy trying to solve things on our own that it doesn't even occur to us to ask for help.

When you think about it, it's really silly. We just keep digging ourselves deeper and deeper into a pit when the best solution—the only solution—is to ask for help. James 1:5 says, "If any of you lacks wisdom, he should ask God, who gives generously to all without finding fault. . . . " God *never* says to us, "How many times do I have to help you? How could you be so stupid? When are you going to learn how to figure things out on your own?"

No, of course not! God understands our limitations better than we do. After all, He created us. He designed us to need Him. The Scripture tells us that God loves to help us. He longs to help us.

Having trouble with your teenager? Ask God to show you what to do. Problems at work? Ask God. Need inspiration for a creative project? Ask God. Whatever situation you face today, God knows exactly what to do. He'll show you—if you just ask Him!

## Take It To Heart!

✍ Is there something you need help with today? Do you have a real problem to solve or a difficult decision to make? Admit that you don't have all the answers and that you need God's help.

✍ Ask God to guide you. Pray for wisdom, insight, and direction. Listen carefully for His response, however it may come to you (a thought, a Scripture, a situation that resolves itself, or words of advice from a trusted friend).

✍ Read Psalm 25:4-5, 9-10; Proverbs 3:5-6; Isaiah 30:21.

# THE SIN
# NOBODY STRUGGLES WITH

A few years ago I was asked to speak to a church group on the subject of materialism. It was a really unusual topic. I titled my message (a little facetiously) "The Sin Nobody Struggles With." In all the years I've attended Sunday school, prayer groups, and Bible studies—in all the times I've counseled with other believers—I've never heard anyone confess to struggling with the sin of materialism.

I mean, people confess to all kinds of hideous sins—but materialism? Oh no! That's those people with the air-conditioned doghouses and gold-plated commodes. It seems that no matter how "comfortably" we live, we can always point to others whose luxurious lifestyle exceeds our own. Now *they* have a problem.

But the truth is, materialism is not defined by how much you have—it's how much it means to you. You can live in a mansion and care nothing for your worldly possessions. You can live in a mud hut and be absolutely obsessed with material things—what you have and don't have, what you wish you had, what your neighbors have. It's not what's in your bank account; it's what's in your heart.

If you're focused on accumulating earthly possessions—

spending money on things you don't need or can't really afford, envying the lifestyle of others, constantly lusting after things you want but don't have—then you've got a problem with materialism. In Luke 12:15 Jesus said, "Watch out! Be on your guard against all kinds of greed; a man's life does not consist in the abundance of his possessions."

Don't let your heart be consumed with preserving or accumulating things. Worldly possessions are only temporary and will one day be destroyed. Instead, focus on things of eternal value. Store up for yourself treasures in heaven, spiritual blessings and rewards that can never be destroyed.

## Take It To Heart!

✍ Take a moment to examine your own heart. Honestly, do you ever struggle with the sin of materialism? Do the things you own really own you?

✍ Ask God to set your heart free. Pray for strength to let go of the things that weigh you down and keep you from serving Him wholeheartedly.

✍ Read Matthew 6:19-21; 1 John 2:15-17; Philippians 4:11b-13.

# SAFELY HOME

Have you ever heard it said that only the good die young? It's an expression that reflects a painful truth: There are so many things in life that just don't make sense. So often it seems that the best and brightest are taken from the world far too soon, and we're left to wonder why.

Somehow it's especially difficult for us when the person is a precious believer. How could God let such a good person die? He or she loved the Lord and served Him faithfully. Why didn't He spare the person? It's a question people have grappled with since the beginning of time.

Isaiah 57:1 sheds some light on the question and gives us at least one answer: "The righteous perish, and no one ponders it in his heart; devout men are taken away, and no one understands that the righteous are taken away to be spared from evil. Those who walk uprightly enter into peace; they find rest as they lie in death."

Sometimes when God allows His saints to die "prematurely," He *is* rescuing them from a world of evil. He's keeping them from future pain and suffering. There may be things we wish they could have lived to see. But there are also things we may be glad they *didn't* see. God may have been protecting them from untold dangers that lay in their path. They will never again be threatened by sin and darkness.

It's not easy to come to terms with the loss of a loved one. It's hard to let go of people we respect and admire. But we can draw comfort and encouragement from knowing that these special people are now safe at home, in the arms of their heavenly Father.

## Take It To Heart!

☙ As you read these words, who comes to mind? Loved ones you have lost? Heroes or victims whose stories made the headlines? People you have never met, but whose lives touched yours in some way?

☙ Thank God for the blessing these people were during their lives here on earth. Imagine the glorious reunion we will all have in heaven one day.

☙ Read Psalm 116:15 and Revelation 21:1-4.

# FOR SUCH A TIME
# AS THIS

The book of Esther tells the fascinating story of an orphaned Jewish girl who, through a miraculous series of events, is chosen to be the bride of King Xerxes—ruler of the Babylonian Empire. Esther's cousin Mordecai learns of a plot to annihilate the entire Jewish race. He calls on Esther to approach the king on behalf of her people, to beseech him for mercy and protection.

At first the young queen is flabbergasted at the thought. She is completely overwhelmed by the magnitude of the request—the risk involved in approaching her notoriously temperamental husband, the doubtful outcome. It could literally cost her life. But Esther's cousin admonishes her to recognize the responsibility that comes with privilege. To whom much is given, much will be required (Luke 12:48). In Esther 4:14, Mordecai asks a pointed question: "Who knows but that you have come to royal position for such a time as this?"

As the story unfolds, it becomes clear that Mordecai is right. God Himself has allowed Esther to become queen—placed her in the palace—for this very moment. He has a plan to deliver His people, and He will use Esther to accomplish it.

The Bible tells us that God has a plan and a purpose for each one of our lives. At times we may feel overwhelmed by the challenges we face. The task we've been given seems too hard, the cost too high. But we must remember that we've been blessed with the incredible privilege of being servants of the Most High. And God has put us where we are for a reason. When we look to Him, He will give us all the wisdom and strength we need to accomplish His purposes. For we, too, are called—for such a time as this.

## Take It To Heart!

✍ What is God calling you to do today? It may be sharing your faith with a coworker, fighting a spiritual battle, restoring a relationship, sacrificing something precious to you, or stepping out in faith. What are you going to do about it?

✍ Ask God to clearly reveal the next step in His plan for you—and give you grace to walk in His will.

✍ Read 1 Peter 2:9 and Joshua 1:9.

# THE DEVIL
# MADE ME DO IT

In 1971 a man named Gerald Mayo filed suit against "Satan and His Staff" in the U.S. District Court in Pennsylvania, alleging that "Satan has on numerous occasions caused the plaintiff misery against the will of the plaintiff, and that Satan has deliberately placed obstacles in his path and has caused the plaintiff's downfall. Plaintiff alleges that by reason of these acts Satan has deprived him of his constitutional rights."[7]

The suit was thrown out when Mayo failed to provide the U.S. Marshal with instructions on how and where to serve Satan's subpoena. Too bad! Many of us would have loved to join Mayo and make it a class action suit.

There's no doubt Satan has caused a world of trouble for us all. The Scripture says he prowls about "like a roaring lion looking for someone to devour" (1 Peter 5:8). Often we feel helpless against his onslaught.

But we're not pitiful victims, doomed to succumb to his wiles. No, we are more than conquerors through Him who loved us. First John 3:8 explains, "The reason the Son of God appeared was to destroy the devil's work." Jesus paid the penalty of our sin for us and set us free from its bondage.

Romans 8:1 tells us, "There is now no condemnation for those who are in Christ Jesus, because through Christ Jesus the law of the Spirit of life set me free from the law of sin and death." We are no longer bound to go on living in sin. The devil can't make us do anything. On the contrary, the Scripture says if we resist him, he'll flee from us (James 4:7). Every one of us has the freedom to choose to walk in obedience to God's Word.

## Take It To Heart!

🕸 When you feel guilty—convicted of your sin—do you take responsibility for your actions? Or do you look for someone or something else to blame?

🕸 Ask God for forgiveness for the times you have given in to temptation and blamed others for your sin. Take responsibility. Pray for strength to resist the devil and stand firm in your faith.

🕸 Read 1 John 4:4; Romans 6:12-14, 18; Titus 2:11-14.

# CAT ON A HOT
# STOVE LID

American author Mark Twain once observed, "We should be careful to get out of an experience only the wisdom that was in it—and stop there, lest we be like the cat that sits on a hot stove lid. She will never sit down on a hot stove lid again—and that is well, but also she will never sit down on a cold one anymore."[8]

I think he has a great point. As believers many of us really try to learn from our experiences. We want to grow and mature in our faith. But sometimes in our eagerness, we walk away with the wrong lesson.

Maybe we were a little too enthusiastic—okay, maybe even pushy or preachy—in our initial attempt to lead a loved one to the Lord. That doesn't mean we should never try to witness to anyone again. Maybe our efforts in one area or another have turned out badly. It doesn't necessarily mean that we aren't called or gifted in that area. Perhaps we missed God's direction and took a wrong turn. Or maybe it was the right turn after all. We just didn't expect the road to be so rough.

It's good to be reflective. The Scriptures tell us that a prudent man gives thought to his ways (Proverbs 14:8, 15). But the Bible also reminds us that, as human beings, our knowledge and understanding is limited. We don't see the whole picture. That's why, when we evaluate any experience, we need to pray for discernment. We must ask God to show us what He wants us to learn from it. Psalm 25:9 says, "He guides the humble in what is right and teaches them his way."

## Take It To Heart!

✍ How do you usually respond to and evaluate an experience? Do you rely on "gut" feelings or instinct? The input of trusted friends?

✍ Ask God to give you wisdom and understanding so that you may learn only what is right and true—the things He wants to teach you.

✍ Read 1 Kings 3:5-10 and John 14:15-17, 26.

# Nana's Poem

E ven though I was just a child, I could tell that it was a very special book. I remember my grandmother always kept it with her Bible. She read from the little devotional so often that eventually the binding cracked, and the cover fell apart. She patched it up and recovered it with a scrap of wallpaper—from the beautiful pink rose pattern she had just used to paper her sitting room. It looked kind of funny, but the book was precious to her.

My grandmother's love and devotion to God made such an impact on my life. As a teenager, when I renewed my own commitment to Christ, I began to have my own personal devotions or quiet time with God. I asked my grandmother for a copy of the book she loved so much (*Streams in the Desert* by L. B. Cowman). Later I discovered that she had underlined her favorite passage for me, quoting a poem by Annie Johnson Flint.

As I look back on my grandmother's life—all that God brought her through—I can see why those words meant so much to her. They mean a great deal to me today. I'd like to share them with you:

> *He giveth more grace when the burdens grow greater,*
> *He sendeth more strength when the labors increase;*
> *To added affliction He addeth His mercy,*
> *To multiplied trials, His multiplied peace.*

*When we have exhausted our store of endurance,*
*When our strength has failed ere the day is half done,*
*When we reach the end of our hoarded resources,*
*Our Father's full giving is only begun.*

*His love has no limit, His grace has no measure,*
*His power has no boundary known unto men;*
*For out of His infinite riches in Jesus,*
*He giveth and giveth and giveth again!*
ANNIE JOHNSON FLINT (1866-1932)

## Take It To Heart!

❧ Do you ever feel as if you're at the end of your rope? What things are weighing on your heart today?

❧ Memorize the words of Flint's poem or one of the Scriptures below. Say it often, especially when you feel that you're losing your grip. Ask God for His grace and strength to see you through.

❧ Read 2 Corinthians 12:7-10; Isaiah 40:28-31; Philippians 4:19.

# But They Don't
# Deserve It

You know, compared to the others, Jonah was one of the most successful prophets in the Bible. Sure, at first he tried to run from God, and there was that unfortunate incident with the big fish. But once he got to Nineveh and preached the word God gave him, Jonah was a *huge* success. These people actually listened to him, instead of stoning him to death or sawing him in half. More than that, they repented of their sin. All of them did—the king and everyone. You'd think God's prophet would be thrilled with the results.

But not Jonah. He actually had the nerve to be angry with God for *forgiving* them. He complained about God being so "gracious and compassionate . . . slow to anger and abounding in love" (Jonah 4:2).

"I knew this would happen," he said. It seems that Jonah wanted God to destroy the city. He wanted to see those wicked people get what they deserved. I guess he forgot that if God had taken that attitude with him, he'd still be at the bottom of the ocean. God forgave *him* when *he* repented. But Jonah was annoyed when God gave the people of Nineveh a second chance.

Now lest we be too quick to judge old Jonah, let's take a look inside our own hearts. Are we ever anxious to see other people suffer the consequences of their actions? Do we sometimes pray that they'll repent and yet secretly hope they'll get what they deserve? If we do, then shame on us. Having experienced God's mercy and grace in our own lives, let us be quick to rejoice when He offers it to others.

## Take It To Heart!

⌇ Think of times when you have experienced God's mercy and forgiveness—times when you didn't get what you deserved.

⌇ Ask God to help you extend that same mercy and forgiveness to others. Pray sincerely that they will repent and be restored and rejoice when that prayer is answered.

⌇ Read Matthew 5:7, 43-48; Romans 4:13; Titus 3:3-7.

# WHAT'S IN YOUR
# BUCKET?

S omeone once said that the human heart is like a bucket. When it gets bumped, whatever's inside comes splashing out! In other words, our hearts are revealed by the way we respond to life's challenges.

I can't think of a better biblical example than the story of Job in the Old Testament. God allowed Satan to bring calamity and disaster upon this righteous man to test him and prove his heart. In one day Job lost all of his herds and flocks, the source of his wealth. His camels, sheep, oxen, donkeys—they were all stolen by raiders or destroyed by fire. At the same time, all of Job's ten children were killed when the house they were staying in collapsed on them.

As Job heard report after report of ruin and loss, the Bible says he fell to the ground in worship. Not in bitterness, not in rage, not in suicidal grief—in *worship*. He said, "The LORD gave and the LORD has taken away; may the name of the LORD be praised" (Job 1:21). He did not sin by charging God with wrongdoing. Instead, he acknowledged God's sovereignty and affirmed his faith in Him.

Job passed the test. His heart proved true. It's obvious

that Job's bucket was full of faith and trust and peace—a spirit of humble submission to the will of God.

What about you? When life bumps your bucket, what comes spilling out? When things don't go your way, when you're faced with an unexpected challenge or a difficult situation, how do you respond?

It's something to think about today.

## Take It To Heart!

📖 What does your response to hardship reveal about the condition of your heart? Are there attitudes or thought patterns you need to change? How could you make those changes?

📖 Ask God to show you how to fill your heart with things that are good and true—things that build your faith and help you stay focused on what's really important in life.

📖 Read Matthew 12:33-35; Psalm 19:14; 34:1; 2 Corinthians 10:4-5.

# STILL A SECRET

There's something about a secret that fires up our imag-
ination and drives our curiosity wild. We've got to
know the answer. We just have to figure it out.

You know, for centuries Christians have been trying to
figure out one of the biggest secrets of all time: the exact date
of Jesus' return to earth. Believers of every generation since
the cross have been convinced that they were living in the end
times and that the Second Coming was imminent.

In Matthew 24:36 Jesus said, "No one knows about that
day or hour, not even the angels in heaven, nor the Son . . .
only the Father." But that hasn't kept Bible scholars from
spending hours upon hours trying to figure it out with for-
mulas and flow charts, complicated calculations and secret
codes.

Many times over it's been announced that the secret day
has been revealed. Somehow the precise moment of Jesus'
return has been discovered. But those days have all come and
gone, with no sign of Him yet.

It's easy to get caught up in the excitement of "solving
the puzzle," uncovering the mystery. But the Scriptures make
it clear that the point is not to try to figure out *when*—but
to be ready *whenever*. So that whether we finish out our days
upon earth or suddenly rise to meet Him in the air, He'll have

found us faithfully serving Him in the work He has called us to do.

We'll have no regrets, and our hearts will be able to say without hesitation, "Even so, come, Lord Jesus!" (Revelation 22:20 NKJV).

## Take It To Heart!

🕭 If you knew that Jesus was coming back tomorrow or next month or at the end of this year, would it change how you live today? In what way?

🕭 Ask God to help you live every day as if it were your last opportunity to accomplish something for His kingdom. Pray that He will show you how to make each day count for eternity.

🕭 Read Matthew 24:26-51 and Matthew 25:1-13.

# WHERE'S THE FRUIT?

Years ago a clever commercial featured a little old lady ordering a hamburger in a fast-food restaurant. When the burger arrived, she lifted the top of the bun, only to find a tiny gray speck where she expected the meat. Remember her question?

"Where's the beef?"

You know, if that sweet, little old lady could examine the body of Christ today, I think she'd have a different question: "Where's the fruit?"

In John 15:16 Jesus said, "I chose you and appointed you to go and bear fruit—fruit that will last." Fruit is the product of something, the result. In this case, it's the natural—or rather supernatural—evidence of God's Spirit working in us. Galatians 5:22-23 tells us what this fruit looks like: "The fruit of the Spirit is love, joy, peace, patience, kindness, goodness, faithfulness, gentleness and self-control."

Unfortunately, this fruit is often sadly lacking. The church is not practicing what it preaches—too many Christians are living like unbelievers. We're not staying connected to the True Vine (John 15:1). There's so little difference between us and the world, it's no wonder we have little impact on our culture. And it's not surprising that non-Christians don't find anything attractive or intriguing about our faith.

Brothers and sisters, this should not be. In Ephesians 4:22-24, the apostle Paul writes, "You were taught, with regard to your former way of life, to put off your old self, which is being corrupted by its deceitful desires; to be made new in the attitude of your minds; and to put on the new self, created to be like God in true righteousness and holiness." Further on he adds, "You were once darkness, but now you are light in the Lord. Live as children of light (for the fruit of the light consists in all goodness, righteousness and truth) and find out what pleases the Lord. Have nothing to do with the fruitless deeds of darkness . . ." (Ephesians 5:8-11).

We've got to let our light shine and our fruit grow—so that the world may know that Jesus lives.

## Take It To Heart!

☞ Is the fruit of the Spirit readily apparent in your life today? Can your friends and family see evidence of your relationship with Christ? Are they drawn to Him because of what they see in you?

☞ Surrender every area of your life to the lordship of Christ. Ask Him to weed out those things that hinder spiritual growth, that He may produce in your life a bountiful harvest of good fruit.

☞ Read John 15:4-8 and Colossians 1:9-14.

# SINGING ON KEY

When we see people who are sad or depressed or discouraged, often our first impulse is to try to cheer them up somehow. If they've got a problem, we want to tell them how to fix it. If they're hurting, we want to say something that will make their pain go away. But in our effort to help them "think happy thoughts," we often do more harm than good.

If you've ever experienced a tragic loss, you know it doesn't help to be told:

"It's all for the best."

"You'll get over it."

"It could be worse!"

"You'll find a new husband (or wife). There are other fish in the sea."

"You can have more children."

As Proverbs 25:20 (NLT) so eloquently puts it, "Singing cheerful songs to a person whose heart is heavy is as bad as stealing someone's jacket in cold weather or rubbing salt in a wound." Instead, the Scriptures tell us to weep with those who weep, mourn with those who mourn (Romans 12:15). Be sensitive to what they're going through. Hurting people don't need our sage advice as much as they need our sympathy and love. They don't need pious platitudes to cheer them up. They need the assurance that they are not alone—that others have been where they are and understand their pain.

Second Corinthians 1:3-4 says, "Praise be to the God and Father of our Lord Jesus Christ, the Father of compassion and the God of all comfort, who comforts us in all our troubles, so that we can comfort those in any trouble with the comfort we ourselves have received from God."

When you don't know what to say, remember what has ministered to you in your time of need. Ask the Holy Spirit to show you how to help. Sometimes the best comfort of all comes in the form of a hug or a listening ear, a friend who will cry with us and pass the tissues.

## Take It To Heart!

𝕯 Name some hurting people in your life today—coworkers, family, friends. How have you reacted or responded to their pain?

𝕯 Ask God to give you wisdom and sensitivity as you reach out to these people. Think of ways you can gently express your love and concern.

𝕯 Read Proverbs 12:18 and Matthew 5:3-9.

# Better or Best?

Luke 10:38-42 tells the story of two sisters who made two very different choices when it came to the way they honored a special houseguest. Martha was thrilled to have the opportunity to play hostess to Jesus and His disciples. She went all out with the preparations, determined to have everything "just so." And who could blame her? This was, after all, a pretty momentous occasion. It's not every day that the Son of God—the Messiah—comes to visit.

But in the midst of the hustle and bustle, Martha's sister Mary was conspicuously absent. Instead of helping Martha turn their humble abode into House Beautiful, Mary was just lounging around—or so it seemed to Martha. She found Mary sitting at Jesus' feet, listening to Him as He taught His disciples.

Naturally, Martha was furious at Mary's "laziness," and she complained to Jesus about it. "Tell her to help me!" But Jesus didn't rebuke Mary. He rebuked Martha: "Martha, Martha . . . you are worried and upset about many things, but only one thing is needed. Mary has chosen what is better . . ." (Luke 10:41-42).

There's certainly nothing wrong with keeping your house in order or with taking special care to make a guest feel welcome. But in her quest for domestic perfection, Martha had gotten carried away, distracted by all the details. In doing so, she had neglected her guest—the very person for whom all the preparations were intended. She was busy doing *for* Him instead of being *with* Him.

You know, you and I need to be careful not to make that same mistake. We mustn't get so busy doing *for* God that we neglect to spend time *with* Him. That precious love relationship is the reason He created us in the first place. Nothing could be more important!

## Take It To Heart!

✍ List some of the things you do for God: participating in various ministries and church activities, volunteering, etc. How much time do these things take? Do the activities ever keep you so busy that you don't have time to focus on your relationship with God Himself?

✍ Don't let good things keep you from what is best. Spend some time alone with God right now—talking to Him, listening to Him, 'sitting at His feet.' Ask Him to help you identify His priorities for you. Pray for wisdom as you determine which things you have been called to do and which things are distractions.

✍ Read Revelation 2:2-5; Psalm 46:10; Psalm 84:1-2, 10.

# THE MOTHER OF
# ALL LIVING VERSUS THE
# FATHER OF LIES

It sounded like an innocent question. The serpent asked Eve, "Did God really say, 'You must not eat from any tree in the garden?'" But the serpent was crafty—more crafty than any of the creatures God had made. He skillfully drew the unsuspecting woman into a conversation that would lead to deadly results.

Eve obligingly explained God's command and the consequence of eating from the tree of the knowledge of good and evil. But the serpent contradicted her. "You will not surely die," he hissed. "For God knows that when you eat of it your eyes will be opened, and you will be like God, knowing good and evil" (Genesis 3:4-5).

Wait a minute, Eve. Think about it: What is the serpent really saying here? God is wrong. He's untruthful. He can't be trusted. The serpent is claiming that God would deliberately withhold something good from His children out of spite. In other words, "God knows this is really good, and He doesn't want you to have it." The accusation is that God is unjust and unfair, egotistical, unwilling to share.

Over the years Satan's strategy hasn't changed much. He whispers the same things to our hearts today. He takes any and every opportunity to malign the character of God and undermine our faith in Him. In John 8:44 Jesus said the devil "was a murderer from the beginning, not holding to the truth, for there is no truth in him. When he lies, he speaks his native language, for he is a liar and the father of lies."

Don't make the same mistake Eve made. In your own life today turn a deaf ear to the devil's lies and hold fast to what you know is true.

## Take It To Heart!

🍂 Do you ever feel disappointed in or disillusioned with God? When your heart is hurting, do you entertain negative thoughts like those described above? If so, write these down and use a concordance to find Scripture that refutes them. Have you let the enemy of your soul drive a wedge between you and your heavenly Father?

🍂 Ask God to help you prepare a battle plan of your own. Think of some strategies you can use to stay on track.

🍂 Read Deuteronomy 32:3-4; Psalm 18:30; 1 John 4:7-10; Romans 8:32.

# ANSWERING
# THE CALL

It's a familiar scene repeated often in sitcoms, cartoons, and movies. A commander summons his troops and calls for volunteers for a difficult and dangerous mission. He asks prospective volunteers to take one step forward. But instead everyone takes one step back. Well, almost everyone. Some unfortunate character hasn't been paying attention. He didn't move fast enough. Now that he's one step in front of everyone else, he's hailed as the lone volunteer.

Although it's played for laughs, it illustrates a somewhat painful truth. Too often in life when leadership is called for—when help is needed—nobody volunteers. No one steps up to the plate.

What a contrast to the scene described in Isaiah 6:8. The Lord of Hosts issues a call for a volunteer to take a message to His people. God asks, "Whom shall I send? And who will go for us?" The prophet Isaiah doesn't hesitate for a moment. Immediately he replies, "Here am I. Send me!"

It would not be an easy task. The first message God gave him was a word of judgment and rebuke. It did not make Isaiah a popular man. But he was a passionate man—a man willing and eager to serve the Lord, no matter what the cost.

He understood the need to proclaim God's truth and call the people to repentance—to give them the opportunity to return to God and be saved.

The call Isaiah answered still goes out today. God is looking for volunteers who will take a stand for Him and carry His truth to the nations. He seeks people who are willing to lay down their lives if necessary for the one who laid down His life for them.

Will you answer the call?

## Take It To Heart!

✐ Have you ever made yourself fully available to God? Think of what you might offer Him: List your time and talents, energy and resources.

✐ Pray for specific people or people groups who need to hear the good news of the gospel. Ask God what He would have you do to reach these people. Be open to whatever He says.

✐ Read Isaiah 52:7; Matthew 9:35-38; Matthew 28:18-20.

# DON'T SHOW UP
# EMPTY-HANDED

The Bible talks a lot about rewards stored up in heaven for the righteous—the blessings that await those who labor tirelessly for the kingdom of God, enduring suffering and persevering in the faith. The apostle Paul often referred to the gift of salvation and these heavenly rewards as "the crown of life" or "the crown of glory" or "the crown of righteousness."

As a child, I was mystified when I heard the grownups at church exclaim how they looked forward to receiving their crowns. Especially when they said they couldn't wait to lay them at Jesus' feet, like the elders in Revelation 4:9-11. Now wait just a minute: You mean you suffer and struggle and sacrifice for the Lord throughout your earthly life, and all you get to show for it is a crown? And then you don't even get to keep it—you have to give it back? It didn't sound like much of an incentive to me.

Then one day the truth dawned on me. If you've ever accidentally shown up at a birthday party or a baby shower or a potluck *empty-handed*, you know the feeling of embarrassment or regret. You desperately wish you had brought a gift.

Well, every one of us has been invited to the greatest celebration of all time—the wedding supper of our heavenly Bridegroom. When we get to heaven and stand in the presence of Jesus—when we see Him face to face—we will fall on the ground in worship. Once we truly realize who God is and how much He has loved us, our hearts will be bursting to love Him in return. As we fully comprehend His sacrifice—what He gave for us—we will want desperately to give Him something in return.

All we will have to give Him is what He has given us— those beautiful crowns. The more faithful and diligent and persevering we are in the here and now, the greater our reward will be in heaven, and the more we will have to give back to honor our beloved Savior.

Let's press on together. Time is short, and we don't want to show up empty-handed.

## Take It To Heart!

ॐ Do you ever stop and think about the reward God has promised us? Are you running the race of faith "in such a way as to win the prize"?

ॐ Ask God to help you live your life in the light of eternity, making the most of the time you've been given. Pray for opportunities to demonstrate your love for Him.

ॐ Read 1 Corinthians 9:24-25; 2 Timothy 4:7-8; James 1:12.

# DROP THE STONE!

There's a powerful scene in John 8 where Jesus is con-
fronted by the Pharisees and teachers of the law. They
bring to Him a woman caught in adultery, and they remind
Him that the Law of Moses says she should be stoned to
death. But when they ask Jesus what He thinks of the matter, He replies simply, "If any one of you is without sin, let
him be the first to throw a stone at her." The Scripture says,
"Those who heard began to go away one at a time, the older
ones first . . ." (John 8: 9).

"The older ones first"—have you ever noticed that?
Why did the older ones leave first? I think it's because the
older we get, the more experience we have in the battle of the
flesh. When we're young—physically or spiritually—we're
full of enthusiasm and zeal and arrogance. We're caught up
in the pride of youth, confident in our own strength, and
intolerant of others' weaknesses.

But those who have matured in years or in faith have
come to realize just how weak and frail human flesh really
is, the depths to which our sin nature will sink. We understand the struggle, the frustration. We've been repeatedly
humbled by our own failures, and so we learn not to be so
quick to condemn others. There but for the grace of God
are we.

Jesus brought the Pharisees up short when He reminded them of this truth. They were convicted of the sinfulness of their own hearts. They knew they had no right to condemn anyone else. So they dropped their stones and went home.

May God grant us the wisdom and humility to "drop the stones" we carry.

## Take It To Heart!

🕮 Are you quick to pass judgment on other people? In what ways? Do you find yourself feeling superior to those whose sin is more blatant or obvious? Why?

🕮 Ask God to forgive you for your self-righteous attitude. Ask Him to help you see yourself as you really are. Pray for a spirit of humility and compassion toward others who are trapped in sin.

🕮 Read Matthew 7:1-5; James 4:11-12; Micah 6:8.

# THE TRAIN TICKET

Corrie was only six when she first began to understand the reality of suffering and death. She had been to the home of a neighbor who had lost a child to illness. For the first time it occurred to Corrie that the members of her family could die. She was so distressed that she couldn't eat or sleep. At the sight of her father coming home from work, she burst into tears. "I need you," Corrie sobbed. "You can't die. You can't."

Her father sat down beside her and said gently, "Corrie, when you and I go to Amsterdam, when do I give you your ticket?"

Corrie thought for a moment. "Why, just before we get on the train."

"Exactly," said her father. "And our wise Father in heaven knows when we're going to need things, too. Don't run out ahead of Him, Corrie. When the time comes that some of us will have to die, you will look into your heart and find the strength you need—just in time."[9]

That strength came to Corrie decades later when she, her father, and sister Betsie were arrested for hiding Jews in their home during the Nazi occupation of Holland. Just in time God gave Corrie the strength that would sustain her through the horrors of the concentration camps and the terrible deaths of her father and sister. It was this supernatural measure of grace and strength that then empowered her, as an elderly woman, to travel all over the world preaching the gospel to millions of people, proclaiming the truth: "There is no pit so deep, that the love of God is not deeper still."

We don't have to live in fear of what the future holds or how we will face the challenges that lie ahead. No matter what happens, our heavenly Father will always be right there beside us. And we will find, as Corrie did, that He will give us all the strength and courage we need—right when we need it.

## Take It To Heart!

𐤃 Do you ever wonder what the future holds? Do you worry about how you would handle this crisis or that disaster? Do you fear what might happen to you?

𐤃 Remember that God is in control. He has promised that He will never leave you nor forsake you. Bring all of your worries and fears to Him. Ask Him to fill your heart with peace as you trust in Him.

𐤃 Read Matthew 6:34; Philippians 4:6-7, 19; Isaiah 43:1-2; Hebrews 4:16.

# WHO CAN ARGUE?

I n *Reader's Digest* a man wrote that he was waiting in line at the bookstore when he happened to glance at the person in front of him. The customer was purchasing a couple of recent best-sellers: *Conversations with God* and *How to Argue and Win Every Time.*

Well, if we're perfectly honest, many of us would have to admit that we've had more than a few "conversations" with God that turned into arguments. Perhaps we're not happy about the direction our lives have taken. Maybe we're angry about something God has or hasn't done.

But you can't argue with God and win—not any time. Isaiah 45:9-12 points out that it's ridiculous even to try. The Most High God must be approached with reverence and respect. This passage says:

> *Does a clay pot ever argue with its maker? Does the clay dispute with the one who shapes it, saying, "Stop, you are doing it wrong!" Does the pot exclaim, "How clumsy can you be!" How terrible it would be if a newborn baby said to its father and mother, "Why was I born? Why did you make me this way?" This is what the LORD, the Creator and Holy One of Israel, says: "Do you question what I do? Do you give me orders about the work of my hands? I am the one who made the earth and created people to live on it. With my hands I stretched out the heavens. All the millions of stars are at my command." (NLT)*

Kind of puts things in perspective, doesn't it? God can do whatever He wants with us. How thankful we should be that He's not only almighty—He's the very definition of goodness, mercy, and love.

## Take It To Heart!

✍ Do you ever find yourself arguing with God? Where does the anger or frustration come from?

✍ Ask God to forgive you for the times that you've been disrespectful or defiant in your attitude toward Him. Humble yourself before Him now. Remember who He is and praise Him for it.

✍ Read Psalm 47; Romans 11:33-36; Ephesians 3:14-21.

# IT'S NOT WHAT I ASKED FOR

As a child, did you ever have a disappointing Christmas? You know, one where you didn't get what you asked for. You were expecting a shiny new bike or a doll or a pony, and what you got was underwear and socks. What were Mom and Dad thinking?

Matthew 7:11 assures us that our Father in heaven knows how to give "good gifts to those who ask him." But He doesn't always give us what we ask *for*. Because He is all-wise, all-knowing, because He is good, because He loves us—He sometimes overrules our requests. He may give us what we need rather than what we want, or what we really and truly want but don't know enough to ask for it.

Like a child on Christmas morning, we may be tempted to pout when the answers to our prayers don't appear as we expected them. But God doesn't make mistakes. His gifts are always perfect. Consider the words of an anonymous Civil War soldier:

> *I asked God for strength, that I might achieve,*
> *I was made weak, that I might learn humbly to obey.*
> *I asked for health, that I might do greater things,*
> *I was given infirmity, that I might do better things.*

*I asked for riches, that I might be happy,*
*I was given poverty, that I might be wise.*
*I asked for power, that I might have the praise of men,*
*I was given weakness, that I might feel the need of God.*
*I asked for all things, that I might enjoy life,*
*I was given life, that I might enjoy all things.*
*I got nothing that I asked for—but everything I had hoped for.*
*Almost despite myself, my unspoken prayers were answered.*
*I am, among all men, most richly blessed.*

## Take It To Heart!

✍ What are some of the things that you have asked God for? Have His answers been what you expected? Explain.

✍ Ask God to help you trust Him even when you don't understand. Pray that He will open your eyes to see the answers to your prayers.

✍ Read Luke 11:1-13 and Romans 8:26-27.

# LABOR OF LIFE

I just love babies! I guess that's why I enjoy watching all those "labor and delivery" programs on the Discovery Channel. Now having watched dozens of women give birth on these shows, I've noticed something. Every one of them approaches labor differently. They use different breathing techniques and positions, different medications and therapies. Some are nervous or fearful; some get angry and upset. Most of them are in a lot of pain. They may sob quietly or let out screams that would wake the dead.

But they all have one thing in common. The moment the baby is placed in the mother's arms, all her distress completely disappears. There is no more panic, no more frustration, no more pain. It's as if the events of the last twenty-four or so hours never even happened. Mom's happiness knows no bounds. She doesn't regret a minute of the experience that enabled her to bring forth life!

Jesus talked about this in John 16:21-22 as He prepared His disciples for His death on the cross. He said, "A woman giving birth to a child has pain because her time has come; but when her baby is born she forgets the anguish because of her joy. . . . So [it is] with you: Now is your time of grief, but I will see you again, and you *will* rejoice, and no one will take away your joy" (emphasis added).

We live in a fallen world full of hurt, disappointment, and heartbreak. But the pain of this life is only temporary. The suffering will not last. One day it will be completely forgotten in the joy we experience when Jesus comes back to take us home with Him. That joy will last forever!

## Take It To Heart!

✍ List some of the problems or heartaches you have to deal with right now that *won't* be an issue in heaven. Then list some of the wonderful things about heaven that you can't wait to experience.

✍ Thank God for the hope of heaven. Ask Him to fill your heart with peace and joy as you put your trust in Him.

✍ Read 1 Corinthians 2:9 and Revelation 21:1-4.

# "SPEAK, LORD!"

There's a story in the Old Testament that is a favorite among Sunday school teachers and little children the world over—the story of a boy named Samuel. From his birth, he was dedicated to the service of God. As a toddler, he was taken to the temple and given to the priests to be trained as a helper in the ministry and worship of the Lord.

While he was still a young boy, Samuel was awakened in the night by a voice calling his name. Thinking it was the high priest, he ran to Eli's room. But the old man had not called him; so Samuel went back to bed.

Three times the voice called him, and three times Samuel went running to Eli. The Scripture explains his confusion, saying that "Samuel did not yet know the LORD. The word of the LORD had not yet been revealed to him" (1 Samuel 3:7).

But when Eli finally realized what was happening, he told the young boy what to do. The next time the voice called, Samuel answered, "Speak, for your servant is listening" (1 Samuel 3:10).

Whenever I read that verse, I'm touched by the innocence of Samuel's childlike faith—unquestioning, unwavering, uncomplicated faith. He was so eager to hear and obey. My heart is broken when I think of the times God has called me, and I failed to recognize His voice. Or worse, refused to listen.

The Scripture says God still calls to us, his servants, today. He has so many wonderful things He longs to share with us. May each one of us choose to respond as Samuel did: "Speak, for your servant is listening."

## Take It To Heart!

🕮 How do you hear God's voice? Does He speak to you during your prayer time? As you read the Scriptures or write in your journal? Maybe He speaks to you as you enjoy the great outdoors or work with your hands. Perhaps you hear Him through your friends and family, as you watch your children or grandchildren at play. Pay attention to the way He speaks most often to *you*.

🕮 Ask God to open your heart to hear what He is saying to you today. Take the time to listen.

🕮 Read John 10:27-28 and Revelation 3:20.

# WHAT DO YOU EXPECT?

The story is told of a couple of identical twins, one an alcoholic and the other a teetotaler. When someone asked the first one why he was an alcoholic, he said, "What do you expect? My father was an alcoholic." When they asked the teetotaler why he wouldn't even *touch* alcohol, he answered, "What do you expect? My father was an alcoholic."

Society tells us that we're all victims: victims of fate, of heredity, or of our DNA. We're doomed to failure because our families, our community, or our culture is dysfunctional. Whatever the problem, it's somebody else's fault.

But the Scriptures make it clear that our circumstances do not determine who we are; how we *respond* to our circumstances does. We can let the challenges of life make us bitter or better. But every one of us has a choice, and we are responsible for the paths we choose.

Deuteronomy 30:11, 16-19 says, "What I am commanding you today is not too difficult for you or beyond your reach. . . . love the LORD your God . . . walk in his ways, and . . . keep his commands, decrees and laws . . . and the LORD your God will bless you. . . . But if your heart turns away and you are not obedient . . . you will certainly be destroyed. . . . I have set before you life and death. . . . Now choose life, so that you . . . may live."

Though He has every right to, God Himself doesn't force us to do anything. He presents us with our options and gives us the opportunity to decide for ourselves. He even tells us what the consequences of our choice will be. Disobedience leads to death. Obedience leads to life.

It's really a no-brainer, isn't it? May each one of us recognize the responsibility we have for the choices we make today—and choose the path that leads to life!

## Take It To Heart!

🍮 Think of some choices that lie before you now. What opportunities do you have today to obey or disobey God's Word? What might the consequences be?

🍮 Ask God to help you accept responsibility for the consequences of bad choices you have made, rather than blaming Him or others. Pray for wisdom and strength as you choose to walk in obedience today.

🍮 Read Psalm 19:7-11; John 5:24; John 10:10.

# WITH HER OWN
# TWO HANDS

Proverbs 14:1 says, "The wise woman builds her house, but with her own hands the foolish one tears hers down." You know, I can't think of any woman who did a more thorough job of destroying her own family than Rebekah.

It started with the birth of her twins, Esau and Jacob. Rebekah favored Jacob. She protected him and looked out for his interests above anything else. And if Jacob was called "the Deceiver," well, he learned a thing or two from his mother.

It was, after all, Rebekah who came up with the elaborate plan to help Jacob deceive his father and brother and steal Esau's birthright. In doing so, Rebekah showed contempt for her husband and a total lack of motherly love and concern for her firstborn. Perhaps she acted out of hurt and bitterness—after years of family squabbles. Or perhaps her intentions were good. Maybe she was just trying to help God along and fulfill in the flesh the prophecy she had received during her pregnancy—that her older son would one day "serve the younger."

But God doesn't need any help. He never rewards scheming and manipulation. Rebekah's deception was exposed. She irreparably damaged her relationship with her husband and her oldest son. And her beloved Jacob had to flee across the country to escape Esau's wrath. She never saw him again. Rebekah tore down her house with her own two hands.

We don't have to make that same mistake today. We can choose to be men and women of integrity—living our lives in a way that pleases God, trusting Him with our families and our future. We can build up our families in an atmosphere of love, honesty, and respect. Then we'll have a "house" to enjoy for years to come.

## Take It To Heart!

☙ Do you ever find yourself trying to manipulate or control members of your family in order to accomplish what you think is best? Are you willing to rationalize or justify sinful behavior (such as dishonesty and deception) if you think it will help the cause?

☙ Ask God to help you be a positive influence in the lives of your loved ones. Don't resort to scheming and manipulation. Surrender every member of your family to God and trust Him to accomplish His will in each of their lives.

☙ Read Proverbs 6:16-19; Galatians 6:7-9; Romans 12:9-21.

# A CHECKERED PAST

Do you have a checkered past? Have you made choices in your life that you deeply regret? Are there things you still struggle with today? Perhaps in your heart of hearts, you long to do great things for God, but you wonder: *How could He possibly use someone like me?*

If you do, guess what? You're in good company. The Bible is chock-full of messed-up, mixed-up people—that God still used! Think about it: Abraham was a coward. Jacob was a liar. Moses was a hothead. Rahab was a prostitute. David was an adulterer. Jonah was a whiner. Matthew was a cheater. Martha was a busybody. Thomas was a doubter. Prior to his conversion, the apostle Paul was a Pharisee who killed Christians in the name of God.

These men and women were all too human. They had serious character flaws. They made major mistakes. But God worked in them and through them to accomplish great and mighty things for His kingdom. In 2 Corinthians 4:7, the apostle Paul explains, "We have this treasure in jars of clay to show that this all-surpassing power is from God and not from us."

He went on to say, "Therefore I will boast all the more gladly about my weaknesses, so that Christ's power may rest on me. That is why, for Christ's sake, I delight in weaknesses, in insults, in hardships, in persecutions, in difficulties. For when I am weak, then I am strong" (2 Corinthians 12:9b-10).

In our weakness, God's power and strength is revealed. Through the cracks in our broken, messed-up lives, His light shines brightly. And the world can see Jesus at work in us. We don't have to be perfect or pious or all together. We just need to be willing and available. Each and every day God uses ordinary people like us to do extraordinary things for Him.

## Take It To Heart!

✍ Are there mistakes in your past or flaws in your character that make you feel inadequate or unfit for service in the kingdom of God? Confess those things to God in prayer. Humbly admit your shortcomings and failures.

✍ Believe what the Word of God says: You can do nothing in your own strength, but His grace *is* sufficient for you. His power is made perfect in weakness (2 Corinthians 12:9). Let Him work in you and through you today.

✍ Read 1 Corinthians 1:26-31 and Psalm 73:23-26.

# NO FISHING

Corrie ten Boom was fond of quoting Micah 7:19, which says that God has cast all our sins into the depths of the sea. Often she would add that He had put up a sign that reads "No Fishing."[10] It's a powerful picture of a truth that can be so hard to grasp.

As Christians we know that God has forgiven our sins. But for some reason we keep fishing them up. We keep reliving the embarrassment and humiliation, the horror of those old sins—over and over again. So often we find ourselves staggering along in our Christian walk, burdened by guilt and regret. God's Word says He has forgotten our sins—so why can't we?

First John 1:9 clearly tells us, "If we confess our sins, he is faithful and just and will forgive us our sins and purify us from all unrighteousness." That's a promise we need to stand on today. The Father of Lies wants to fill our hearts with doubt, guilt, and fear. This "enemy of our souls" tries to keep us in bondage to the sins of our past. But this is the time when we need to forget our feelings and cling to the truth of God's Word. The blood of Jesus was shed for us. His blood covers our sin and shame. We've been forgiven. We've been cleansed. We've been set free.

When you find the sins of your past flashing through

your mind today, resist the urge to go fishing. Instead, immediately start praising God for His amazing grace and give Him glory for the forgiveness that is yours in Christ.

## Take It To Heart!

🕊 Are there sins in your past that you continually remember and relive? Does the guilt and shame keep you from experiencing freedom in your walk with Christ?

🕊 Thank God that He really *has* forgiven you—whether you "feel" forgiven or not. Memorize a Scripture you can repeat to yourself whenever the memories come back to haunt you. Stand on the truth of God's Word.

🕊 Read Psalm 103:8-12; Psalm 130:1-4; Zephaniah 3:17.

# JERUSALEM, JERUSALEM

I think it's one of the saddest verses in all of Scripture. I know it breaks my heart every time I read it. In Matthew 23 Jesus is preaching in the temple. Here He is—the Messiah, the anointed one, Israel's long-awaited deliverer. He has come to His own, but His own will not receive Him. They do not recognize Him (John 1:10-11).

Suddenly Jesus says, "O Jerusalem, Jerusalem, you who kill the prophets and stone those sent to you, how often I have longed to gather your children together, as a hen gathers her chicks under her wings, but you were not willing" (Matthew 23:37). He has wanted to embrace them, to draw them tenderly to Himself—but they would not let Him. It's an indescribable tragedy.

Whenever I think of this verse, I'm grieved—not only for the nation that missed their Messiah, but for the times when I myself have stubbornly refused to heed His call. Times when I have persisted in sin, ignored His counsel, denied my dependence on Him, rejected His love, and looked elsewhere for comfort in my pain.

The suffering I experience as a result is entirely my own fault. He would have spared me from it. In His love, He would have gathered me to Himself and kept me from harm's way. If only I had heeded His call. But I would not.

His grief over it is even greater than my own—because His love for me is greater than my own.

God forgive us all! Help us to heed Your call today . . . and come running into Your arms of love.

## Take It To Heart!

✍ Have you ever run from God? Ignored or forgotten Him? Refused His love? Are there things in your life that you insist on doing on your own, in your own way?

✍ Ask God to help you fully surrender your heart and life to Him. Ask Him to forgive you for your stubbornness and self-will. Let Him lavish His love on you today.

✍ Read Joel 2:12-13; Isaiah 1:18; 2 Corinthians 7:10a.

# THE PRAYER OF
# JEHOSHAPHAT

A couple of years ago, there was a lot of interest in a little prayer tucked into the historical record found in First Chronicles—the prayer of Jabez. Some time ago I stumbled across a little verse in *Second* Chronicles—2 Chronicles 20:12. It's quickly become one of *my* favorite Bible prayers.

King Jehoshaphat and his tiny nation found themselves in dire circumstances. Their enemies had gathered a vast army against them and were approaching. The king called the people of Judah to fast and pray. Young and old, men, women, and children—they all gathered at the temple to stand before the Lord.

Jehoshaphat cried out to God, reminding Him of His promise to care for them. He declared the nation's commitment to wait on the Lord for deliverance, and he referred specifically to the crisis at hand—the imminent attack of the enemy. The king concluded his prayer with these simple words: "We do not know what to do, but our eyes are upon you."

So many times I've found myself completely overwhelmed by the circumstances of life. In my prayers for my loved ones, myself, or our nation, I've cried out to God with the words of King Jehoshaphat: "We do not know what to do, but our eyes are upon you."

The Scripture says that those who look to the Lord will never be ashamed. They will not be forsaken. As Jehoshaphat and his people waited on God, they received this precious promise from Him: "Do not be afraid or discouraged because of this vast army. For the battle is not yours, but God's. . . . Stand firm and see the deliverance the LORD will give you" (2 Chronicles 20:15b, 17b).

God offers that same assurance to you and me today.

## Take It To Heart!

🕉 Are you or someone you love faced with an "impossible" situation today?

🕉 Pray the prayer of Jehoshaphat. Shift your focus from your circumstances to the awesome power of Almighty God who fights for you. Stand firm by faith.

🕉 Read Psalm 121:1-8; Isaiah 46:4; 2 Timothy 4:18.

# THE ANSWER IS
# ON THE WAY

Has it ever seemed to you that the "heavens are as brass"—that as your prayers go up, they hit the ceiling and come crashing down again? Maybe you have been waiting and waiting and *waiting* to hear from God about a particular circumstance or situation, but the answer is nowhere in sight. Is God just too busy? Has He forgotten you? Is He even listening? Does He care?

The book of Daniel gives us a startling insight—an amazing behind-the-scenes look—at what goes on when we pray. We can see why sometimes the answers take so long to come our way. In chapter 10 we learn that the prophet Daniel had been fasting and praying for three long weeks, urgently seeking a word from the Lord. It was one of those critical situations where time is of the essence. Why was there no answer?

Suddenly an angel appeared, saying, "Do not be afraid, Daniel. Since the first day that you set your mind to gain understanding and to humble yourself before your God, your words were heard, and I have come in response to them."

The angel goes on to explain, "But for twenty-one days the spirit prince of the kingdom of Persia blocked my way.

Then Michael, one of the archangels, came to help me . . ." (Daniel 10:13 NLT). An epic battle had taken place. Now that the way was clear and the messenger free, Daniel would receive the answer he had been waiting for.

In Ephesians 6 the apostle Paul reminds us of something we often forget—something that is hard for us to truly comprehend: There are spiritual forces at work in the heavenly realms. There is an unseen battle going on all around us.

We can't be fainthearted or easily discouraged when our requests aren't instantly granted. We may be right on the verge of a breakthrough—if we press in and persevere in prayer. It could be that the answer is already on the way.

## Take It To Heart!

✍ Have you been waiting to hear from God? Have you been praying for something or someone without any apparent response?

✍ Don't give up! Persevere in prayer. Ask God to show you how and what to pray as you wait expectantly for His answer.

✍ Read 2 Kings 6:15-17; Isaiah 65:24; 1 Thessalonians 5:16-18.

# DON'T LISTEN

Years ago the saying went, "Sticks and stones can break my bones, but words will never hurt me." Of course we realize now that words are some of the most powerful weapons of all. They can inflict wounds that scar a person for life.

Sometimes the deepest wounds are caused not by a vitriolic tirade but by a thoughtless remark—careless or reckless words from someone who thought we were out of earshot. They didn't really mean anything by it. They weren't trying to hurt us. They didn't think we could hear.

Ecclesiastes 7:21-22 warns us not to let idle words destroy us or our relationships with others: "Do not pay attention to every word people say, or you may hear your servant cursing you—for you know in your heart that many times you yourself have cursed others."

The truth is, we've all spoken thoughtlessly, reacted in anger or frustration, blurted out things we don't mean, or said things we regret or repent of later. Because we ourselves have done these things, the Scriptures tell us we need to be patient and understanding with others, giving them the benefit of the doubt.

Maybe they really didn't mean it. They were just joking around or blowing off steam. Maybe they're hurt or angry or confused. There's something deeper going on that may or may not have anything to do with us.

When someone says something that hurts your feelings, don't be quick to take offense and break off the relationship. Instead, remember the times you yourself have spoken out of turn. Be quick to forgive and look for ways to bring healing and reconciliation.

## Take It To Heart!

℘ Are there people in your life today whose words have hurt you? What about people your words have hurt?

℘ Ask God to help you forgive those who have wounded you. Ask Him to forgive you for wounding others. Pray for restoration and reconciliation in these relationships. Be willing to humble yourself and make the first move.

℘ Read Colossians 3:12-14 and Matthew 6:14-15.

# St. Francis's Paradox

You know, as human beings, we are naturally selfish. We're practically born kicking and screaming and demanding our own way. As believers, we often find that our greatest struggle is to "crucify the flesh." It's so hard to put to death our old nature with its sinful self-absorption, choosing instead to live our lives for the glory of God and in service to our fellow man. But Jesus said, "If anyone would come after me, he must deny himself and take up his cross and follow me" (Matthew 16:24).

Somehow it seems incomprehensible to us that joy and peace and fulfillment come not when we're getting what we want, but when we're giving to others. Not when we're selfish, but when we're selfless. Not when we're demanding our rights, but when we're surrendering them. Not when we're grasping, but when we're letting go.

But in Matthew 10:39, Jesus explained, "Whoever finds his life will lose it, and whoever loses his life for my sake will find it."

St. Francis of Assisi expressed this glorious paradox in a beautiful prayer:

> *O Divine Master, grant that I may not so much seek*
> *To be consoled, as to console,*
> *To be understood, as to understand,*

*To be loved, as to love.*
*For it is in giving that we receive;*
*It is in pardoning that we are pardoned;*
*It is in dying that we are born to eternal life.*

## Take It To Heart!

☞ There are hurting people all around you—people who need comfort, encouragement, and prayer. List the people who come to mind immediately.

☞ Ask God to help you open your eyes to the needs of others and focus on reaching out to them. Spend your prayer time today seeking God on behalf of these people. Look for creative ways to touch their hearts and lives.

☞ Read 1 Corinthians 1:18-31 and Romans 12:9-21.

# A SIMPLE CALL

Do you ever dream of God calling you to a worldwide ministry? Something with serious impact. You're so grateful for all that He's done for you. You wish you could do great things for Him. You want to shout it from the mountaintops, tell everyone on the planet about His amazing love. You'd be willing to make any sacrifice to demonstrate *your* love for Him. If only He would ask you . . .

The Gospel of Mark tells us about a young man who felt this way. He had been possessed by a legion of evil spirits. "Night and day among the tombs and in the hills he would cry out and cut himself with stones" (Mark 5:5). Then Jesus came and set him free. In an instant the demons were gone. The young man was no longer tortured by their presence. The townspeople were amazed when they saw him clothed and in his right mind, sitting at Jesus' feet. No, they were more than amazed—they were terrified! What sort of Man could command that kind of power? They pleaded with Jesus to go away and leave them alone.

As Jesus got into the boat, the young man begged to be allowed to go with Him. He was eager to leave everything behind and follow Jesus—something many of the other disciples had been initially reluctant to do. But Jesus said no. Instead, Jesus gave the young man a different assignment:

"Go home to your family and tell them how much the Lord has done for you" (Mark 5:19).

Some of us are called to the mission field overseas, and some of us are called to the mission field in our own family. After all, our family members are the ones who know us best. They are the ones who see the greatest change in our lives—the incredible difference that a relationship with Christ can make. And their salvation is no less important to Jesus than the millions we will never meet.

Though it may have seemed like a small thing, the Scripture tells us that the young man did just as Jesus asked. Are we willing to do the same?

## Take It To Heart!

🕮 Make a list of the people closest to you who do not know Jesus as their personal Savior. These may include family and friends, neighbors and coworkers.

🕮 Pray for their salvation. Ask God to help you be a good example. Look for opportunities to share your testimony.

🕮 Read Psalm 66:16; 1 Peter 3:15; Matthew 25:21.

# FIGHT TO THE FINISH

It was one of the longest wrestling matches on record. The two powerful men grappled back and forth, each one determined to be the victor in a battle that lasted through the night. By daybreak one of the men realized that there was something supernatural about his mysterious opponent. The man's power and strength were—well—inhuman.

As the sun rose, this opponent suddenly decided to call it quits. "Let me go," he said. But after wrestling with him all night long, Jacob realized he had grabbed on to Someone special. He wasn't about to release his hold. Instead, Jacob insisted, "I will not let you go until you bless me" (Genesis 32:26).

Jacob's determination and persistence—not to mention perception—was well rewarded. His opponent replied, "Your name will no longer be Jacob, but Israel, because you have struggled with God and with men and have overcome" (Genesis 32:28).

Through the long, cold night, Jacob had been wrestling with God Himself. God had tested him. And Jacob had passed the test. In the end, Jacob received the blessing he sought because he wouldn't let go. He wouldn't give in. He wouldn't give up.

You know, sooner or later every one of us will find ourselves face to face with a challenge that tests us to our very limits. In 1 Timothy 6:12a, the apostle Paul urged all of us: "Fight the good fight of the faith. Take hold of the eternal life to which you were called. . . ."

Are you wrestling with something in your life today? Is there a temptation too strong, a crisis too great, a challenge that seems totally insurmountable? Don't be discouraged. You can pass this test. Keep at it. Ask God to give you strength. And don't let Him go until He blesses you!

## Take It To Heart!

🕊 How have you been tested in your walk with Christ? Think of some of the struggles you currently face.

🕊 Pray for strength and patience and perseverance. Think of how you will feel—and all that you will have gained—when you pass this test.

🕊 Read Philippians 3:12-14 and James 1:2-4, 12.

# BENJAMIN FRANKLIN'S EPITAPH

Someone once said, "You know you're getting old when you bend over to tie your shoe and think to yourself, 'What else can I do while I'm down here?'" The comical adage reflects a simple truth: As we get older, our bodies don't work the way they used to. They start falling apart on us. They wear out. Our hearts grow weary, too—weary of the trials and tribulations of this life, weary of the battle between the flesh and the spirit, between the desire to sin and the desire to serve God.

Some people adopt the philosophy that "life is hard, and then you die." But that's not the end of the story, at least not for Christians. The Bible says that one day we will be changed—in a moment, in the twinkling of an eye. The trumpet of the Lord will sound; the dead in Christ will rise, and we will all be instantly transformed. We'll be given brand-new bodies that never grow old, never wear out, never succumb to sin. First Corinthians 15:49 tells us that just as our earthly bodies resemble that of our earthly father, Adam, our heavenly bodies will resemble that of our heavenly Father, God. In other words, they'll be perfect.

One of America's founding fathers anticipated this glo-

rious day when he penned his own epitaph, which was not used on his tombstone but did appear in newspapers at his death. Franklin wrote:

THE BODY
Of
BENJAMIN FRANKLIN
*Printer*
*Like the cover of an old book,*
*Its contents torn out,*
*And stripped of its lettering and gilding*
*Lies here, food for worms;*
*Yet the work itself shall not be lost,*
*For it will (as he believed) appear once more,*
*In a new,*
*And more beautiful edition,*
*Corrected and amended*
BY THE AUTHOR[11]

In that day we who know Christ will live happily ever after!

## Take It To Heart!

𝒟 Do you ever feel old or weary and worn out? Do you ever get discouraged with life and the world in general? Rest in the knowledge that the struggles of this life *will* one day come to an end. Take some time to reflect on the glorious future that awaits in heaven.

𝒟 Ask God to help you remember that this world is not your home—you're just passing through! Pray for strength to keep going for as long as He gives you.

𝒟 Read 1 Corinthians 13: 12; 2 Corinthians 4:16-18; Galatians 6:9.

# NOTES

1. Gary O'Connor, *Ralph Richardson: An Actor's Life* (New York: Applause Books, 2000), 253.

2. Luis Palau, *Experiencing God's Forgiveness* (Sisters, Ore.: Multnomah Press, 1985).

3. Lyrics by Alan Jay Lerner and music by Frederick Loewe, "I'm An Ordinary Man," from the Broadway musical *My Fair Lady*, 1956.

4. Mary Lou Retton, interview with the author, February 24, 1999.

5. Julius Reiger, *The Silent Church: The Problem of the German Confessional Witness* (Norwich, England: SCM-Canterbury Press Limited, 1944).

6. Michelle Akers, interview with the author, August 8, 1998.

7. *Gerald Mayo v. Satan and His Staff*, U.S. District Court, Western District of Pennsylvania, 54 FRD 282, December 3, 1971.

8. Mark Twain, *The Wit and Wisdom of Mark Twain* (Philadelphia: Running Press, 2002), 86.

9. Corrie ten Boom, *The Hiding Place: 25th Anniversary Edition* (Grand Rapids: Baker Books, 1996), 29.

10. Corrie ten Boom, *Tramp for the Lord* (Old Tappan, N.J.: Fleming H. Revell, 1974), 167.

11. William J. Federer, *America's God and Country Encyclopedia of Quotations* (Coppell, Tex.: FAME Publishing, 1995), 253.

CHRISTIN DITCHFIELD is the host of the syndicated radio program *Take It To Heart!*®, heard daily on stations across the United States, Canada, and Central and South America. Using real life stories, rich word pictures, biblical illustrations, and touches of humor, she calls believers to enthusiastically seek after God. She offers practical tools to help people deepen their personal relationship with Christ.

A popular conference speaker and author of more than forty books, Christin has also written dozens of tracts for Good News Publishers, including "Under Attack"—an evangelistic response to the 9/11 tragedy, which has sold more than a million copies worldwide. Her articles have appeared in numerous national and international magazines, including *Focus on the Family*, *Today's Christian Woman*, *Sports Spectrum*, and *Power for Living*.

Christin Ditchfield is the founder and president of Take It To Heart Ministries. To learn more, call (800) 478-4178, write to P.O. Box 1000, Osprey, FL 34229, or visit the ministry website at www.TakeItToHeartRadio.com. Christin often speaks at banquets, conferences, and retreats. For information on scheduling and availability, please contact Speak Up Speaker Services toll free at (888) 870-7719 or e-mail Speakupinc@aol.com.